Prometheus's Torch

Edited by Lorraine Cuddeback

Prometheus's Torch

Edited By Lorraine Cuddeback

Apprentice House
Baltimore, Maryland
www.apprenticehouse.com

ISBN: 978-1-934074-33-6

Printed in the United States of America

First Edition
10 9 8 7 6 5 4 3 2 1

Project Manager: Elizabeth Watson
Cover design: Elizabeth Watson
Internal design: Elizabeth Watson & Brielle Fiorillo
Cover photo credit: Pavel Jedlicka/stock.xchng

Published by Apprentice House
The Future of Publishing...Today!

Apprentice House
Communication Department
Loyola College in Maryland
4501 N. Charles Street
Baltimore, MD 21210

410.617.5265 • 410.617.5040 (fax)
www.ApprenticeHouse.com • info@ApprenticeHouse.com

"An infallible test of civilization is that a man claiming to be civilized should be an intelligent toiler; that he should understand the dignity of labor, and that his work should be such as to advance the interests of the community to which he belongs."

-Gandhi

The Learner's Bill of Rights
Conceived and written by the staff of The Learning Bank of C.O.I.L., Inc.

You have a right to learn.

You have a right to learn at your own level.

You have a right to be involved in deciding what you will learn.

You have a right to make learning a top priority in your life.

You have a right to be patient with yourself.

You have a right to not compare yourself to anyone else.

You have a right to try, and try again if that's what it takes.

You have a right to be discouraged sometimes. Learning is hard work!

You have a right to achieve your goals.

You have a right not to be embarrassed.

You have a right to ask why, if you aren't getting what you want from the learning situation.

Contributors

Learners:
Peggie Gilmore
Leon Lovess
Althea Moore
LaSharon Diggs
Rosa Lee McCray
Charles Murphy
Arthur Thomas Goodin
Bern Davis
Beverly Jackson-Zen
Shannon Baytops
Anthony Brown
Charles Vessells
Janet Obeng
Dana Punnett
Angelo Lewis
Gregory Whisonant
Tyrone Peoples

The Learning Bank Staff:
LeRoy J. Young, Jr.
Yvonne Butler

Acknowledgments

First of all, a great many thanks to the staff of The Learning Bank, most especially to the teachers who let me pull learners from their classes day after day, and who not only encouraged their learners to partake in the project, but on occasion, outright pushed them. A special word of thanks goes to Ms. Yvonne Butler, who has guided me since I stepped foot inside The Learning Bank, and always believed in my ambitions idea for this project.

I next owe my thanks to the staff of the Center for Community Service and Justice at Loyola College, especially Missy Gugerty, who gave me the open opportunity to complete this project.

Many thanks also go to Dr. Kevin Atticks, for allowing me to use Apprentice House to publish, and for not thinking that I was completely insane when I first proposed the book idea to him.

I cannot even begin to list the number of things which Dr. Cinthia Gannett did to help me along with this project. Without her passion and support (and the Loyola Writing Center) I doubt this book would have come to fruition. Also, thanks goes to Josh Kazman and Jen Follett, the consultants at the Writing Center who gave me critical feedback as I drafted and revised.

And last, but not least, to the friends who have read drafts and corrected my often rebellious grammar, especially Matthew Rooney, David Hepburn, Patrick Galloway, Kevin Hughes, and the many others who oiled the gears I needed to write.

♦ Table of Contents

♦ Introducton

If we are to listen to the myths, humanity gained the knowledge of fire before there was time, before we created and imposed the arbitrary markers of seconds, minutes, hours, days, years. Time was told by movement: the speed of a butterfly's wings, or the passing of the sun from the eastern horizon to the western. In this era, humans were slaves to nature – their own, and the rest of creation's. They were hot when the temperature rose; they were cold when the temperature dropped. They could eat only what they gathered, and that only raw; their weapons were only as sharp as the stones that could be found. There was no language, no control over their minds or bodies. Everything was instinct, without the unity or organization which leads to civilization.

Then the giant came, the one called Prometheus. Head and shoulders above his creations, the giant held a large hollow stick, large enough to be a quarterstaff; hidden within was bright light, intense heat. As a thief in the night, Prometheus had gone to the fire on the mountain, the Olympian fire, and with his bare hands – hands that neither scarred nor burned from the fire – placed red-hot coals in long piece of fennel. He did this with smoldering defiance in his eyes, against the law of the Thunderer, Zeus. For Zeus wished to withhold the knowledge of fire from humanity, in order to keep them in the cold darkness of ignorance while the gods alone enjoyed the privilege of the flame. Prometheus would not stand for it; he would see humanity come into its own and flourish.

So Prometheus brought fire to his creations.

And what else? Fire begat knowledge – the knowledge of cooking, of metalworking, of medicine. Humankind was now free to work at night, or to mold metal into sharpened points and blades. More efficient tools created free time – time used for storytelling, for artwork, for culture to build. Language bloomed as knowledge was created – for language grew to pass on that knowledge, to let one another know how to do that, how to get this done. Men and women rose above instinct in the glow of the fire that burned in their camps.

But as humanity began to flourish, Prometheus was punished. A rebel, a revolutionary, he was dangerous to Zeus's regime. So he was chained to a rock, tortured for all of eternity as an eagle (ironically, a future symbol of liberty) ate at his body.

All this, for a few coals of fire. From the marble columns of the Parthenon, to the hardcover textbooks of today, the Prometheus myth has been told and retold to explain humanity's humble beginnings. The story is, on the surface, one about fire; a creation myth which accounts for humankind's evolution. But at the heart of the story are oppression and rebellion, defiance and revolution. Taken literally, every flame we tend to today can be seen as a descendent from that first torch of Prometheus; taken figuratively, we see that the light which Prometheus brought to us was enlightenment. Zeus, who could throw fire upon the people with a bolt of his lightning, had not forbidden the existence of fire so much as the knowledge of how to control it. The prohibition, then, wasn't so much against the torch as it was against the secrets that the torch spilled.

The Greeks who first told this story so many centuries ago knew that knowledge births power. Knowledge does not threaten, but rather the power knowledge brings. We hide truths not because we wish for secrets, but because we fear the power those who know them could have over us. When we say that this person or that person "knows too much for their own good," the hidden ending is usually "and for mine."

This, perhaps, is how education has become a privilege.

Of course, this is America, and there is a public school system – one which is free and open to all regardless of gender, race, and religion. Yet I have found that there is a clear difference between "going to school," and "getting an education;" and I realize this statement then begs the question: but how do they differ?

Here enters The Learning Bank of C.O.I.L., Inc., the learners who attend classes there, and the stories which they have provided for this book. Working with the men and women at The Learning Bank has taught me a great deal; yet the knowledge is of a different sort than I learned from textbooks and workbooks. I underwent a challenging education, an education which questioned – nay, destroyed – my assumptions about life and education in Baltimore. When I first conceived of this project, the aim was to bring the emotional turmoil, sympathy, and compassion I experienced to as many other people as possible. It was, I admit, a somewhat unrealistic aspiration; if for no other reason than I often find it hard to process my experience in my own terms, let alone to explain it to others.

And then it occurred to me: why am I trying to use my story? Why not bring the stories of the learners to the world, if that is what affected me so profoundly?

Of course, the project wouldn't be that simple; the book needed a context, a theme – I needed to say something with this book. So I read books and articles on literacy, education, and philosophy; and the theorist who stood out the most was Paulo Freire. His work has been a strong influence on this collection, and on the themes highlighted within. In the Prometheus myth, I have found the greatest incarnation of Freire's theory of revolution: Prometheus, the member of the ruling class who rebels against their institution. Prometheus who recognizes the need of humankind to become more than mere objects which the forces of nature act upon, and grow into subjects with self-possessed actions. Prometheus who brings fire to humankind: because fire is self-sustaining, a revolution which brings about more revolutions. Fire and light – the traditional symbol of knowledge (on my class ring, a torch signifies my academic honors). Prometheus, who then paid a dear price by becoming oppressed himself, chained and bound and punished for being anything other than the ruling class asked him to be.

In action, the image of Prometheus's torch bearing the dangerous knowledge, which he so boldly gave to humanity, fit in well with my understanding of Freire. Still, there was more to uncover: not just the what of the myth, but the why. This is the same as when we deal with injustice – it is not enough to fight against the empirical results of poverty, because we must also question how the injustice came to be in the first place.

Though the myth doesn't detail Prometheus's motives for his rebellion against Zeus, I would like to believe it is a motive such as Freire imagines: love. Prometheus's love for his creation is, like Freire's love for the human community, ultimately what can overcome the "dehumanization" which is the effect of oppression. Raised Catholic, I cannot help but to agree:

love thy neighbor as yourself, it is said.

Love resounds through this book, the overarching theme that ties together the four sections of this book: Hope, Conversion, Revolution, and Solidarity. In this book, there are women who love their husbands, parents who love their children, and sons and daughters who have loved their parents and grandparents. These loves motivate the men and woman who have contributed here. A grandson wants to prove his grandmother's faith in him, a woman writes a testimony to her faith, and a mother changed her life around for the love of a baby daughter. Love brings us hope, love enacts conversions, love calls us to solidarity, and, if we are to believe Freire, is it love which drives our revolutions: revolutions which are "acts of love against the lovelessness of the oppressors."

Love, then, leads to revolution, and lights up our future. Simply put, in a way which is truthful, though it seems hugely impossible: love is our future. And it is my sincerest hope that you find something to love in the stories here, for these men and woman will be the ones to realize our love-filled future.

🔥 Hope
It's Never Too Late

Retirement. The golden years. Sweet peace, work-free days, relaxation – this is how many of us see our lives when we're older, with grown children and growing grandchildren. We expect hours spent in recliners, playing bridge, or, for the more ambitious, traveling, seeing the world before it's too late to do so.

This is not the case for many of the men and women at The Learning Bank. Some of the most regular students there are over the age of fifty; though most won't tell you exactly how old they are. Most teachers will tell you that the easiest students to work with are those who are older. Older learners come to The Learning Bank by choice, because a GED is something they want for themselves: not because an employer, parole officer or other authority figure told them to get it. Though the men and women in this chapter have had fairly successful jobs, raised families, and lived good lives, they still chose to come back, in the years when they should be enjoying life, to complete their education. Earning a degree is, to these learners, the final torch to light in a lifetime of goals and experiences which are already burning bright.

Acting upon such desire makes each of these men and woman immensely courageous; for it takes a great deal of courage to admit that one isn't literate in today's world, where the ability to read is often taken for granted. It is also a risk – a risk of exposure, yes, but a risk of failure. Readjusting to the cycle of learning, studying, and working after years out of the academic arena is not an easy transition. As children, we can all remember just how much we struggled in September after a summer of freedom; now imagine that the summer was decades long, and maybe we can fathom just how much harder that would make the re-entrance into school. Like turning on a light after being in darkness, the learners' returns can be intimidating, even a little painful until their eyes and mind readjust.

Not all of the learners highlighted in this section are retirement age – LaSharon Diggs is only in her thirties, yet I placed her in this section because after years as a nursing assistant, she wants to push herself for a nursing license. LaSharon's poetry is another kind of risk for her; she uses it to express her emotions, making herself vulnerable to a reader. There is also Althea Moore, who quite frankly told me that she needed her education, needed it to make her "whole." She has risked herself in many ways; Althea had never told her daughter that she didn't graduate high school, and then revealed the truth when it seemed her daughter was on the verge of dropping out. Althea shone a torch on her past, and with that light her daughter was able to avoid the mistakes which Althea had made. At times, the energy Althea spends working, attending classes and caring for a family has impacted her health. There were a number of weeks where I saw her come in for class looking exhausted and unwell, and yet she continued to make her studies a priority.

In some cases, it was family which gave the learner the courage to pursue his or her education. Rosa Lee McCray is following directly in her son's footsteps – he attended The Learning Bank a few years back. The glowing way she spoke of her son's success showed me how she admires him; it was a strange reversal of roles, for me (in many ways, still just a child) to see the parent hold up the child as an example to follow. One could call it a reverse passing of the educational torch.

Peggie Gilmore, the woman who wrote the essay for which this section is titled, also returned with the support of her family – she would love to read to her many grandchildren and great-grandchildren. Yet, ultimately Peggie says she has returned for herself. Her education is the fulfillment of a personal dream, not anyone else's. Leon Lovess echoes this same sentiment – he is back in school to write. Leon has a million stories in his head, and he wants the world to be able to enjoy them as he does. Charles Murphy and Arthur T. Goodin feel the similarly; their degree is a goal they have saved until now, and with little else to hold them back, they are pursuing it with every bit of energy they have – and believe me, they have a lot.

These older learners are the ones who crack jokes with you in class, who help to keep the younger learners in line, who lead by example. Yet, these were also the learners who walked in virtually terrified on the first day of class, because they are afraid of being "too old." Still, they are the ones who teach the teachers: the history behind their stories is astounding. In talking with them, I was given glimpses into a past which was flesh-and-blood, not merely empty words on a textbook page. I heard about the rural south and segregated schools from Arthur; Peggie told me of a time when women were encouraged to drop out young, marry, and have children. These were experiences in education radically different from my own. Outraged though I was to hear Arthur had to buy his own books, and though I was shocked to hear that Peggie wasn't expected to finish school, there was little I could do to change that.

But there is the future. The future, where these learners' grandchildren could (and most did) finish high school. The future, where maybe Leon can publish a story and LaSharon can work as a nurse. The most profound lesson to be learned in these stories is that dreams don't retire.

Peggie Gilmore

One morning, not long after I had begun the interviews for this book, I was approached by Ms. Baxter, a longtime member of the teaching staff at The Learning Bank who was, for the current cycle, teaching a Social Studies class. Ms. Baxter pulled me aside and asked in a low voice: "Have you met Peggie Gilmore?" When I shook my head no, she continued on, "Well, you really should. She's one of my best students, and a great writer, and I would really like her to be a part of this project." And with that, Ms Baxter nudged me towards Peggie, who was casually standing outside a classroom, waiting to enter.

Nervous though I was speaking to her (for it was the first time I had approached someone who hadn't previously expressed interest) I soon found myself sitting across from the red-haired, smiling older woman, as we discussed her family and how she believed that it is "never too late" to fulfill a dream.

As the story goes, Peggie was simply watching television one day – the news, to be precise – when she stumbled upon hope: "I saw an eighty-two year old lady on T.V. that got her GED, so that showed me right there that it is never too late…" Not long after seeing that news report, Peggie enrolled in The Learning Bank, and is now taking reading and math classes to pursue her GED; something she tells me she never considered possible at her age (which, with an arched eyebrow and a wink, she declined to reveal to me).

For all of Peggie's drive and energy, you might not realize that she is a grandmother, and great-grandmother five-times over, as well – with, Peggie told me, her eyes twinkling, one more to come. Peggy has watched all of her grandchildren go through high school, and she has seen the three oldest graduate: one to become an electrician, one to become a registered nurse, and the most recent graduate going to college to become an architect. She has seen how they strive for their dreams; at one time, she thought that was the job of the young, but now she knows that it's "never too late."

"Now," Peggie says, since she has finished helping her family achieve success "it's more important to me than ever to fulfill *my* goals, follow *my* dreams and to accomplish some things that I want to accomplish in my life before I die." Peggie's ultimate ambition for herself is to earn a professional degree – an associate's degree, a bachelor's degree, even a doctorate – something which proves that she is an educated woman, and which shows the world that it doesn't matter what your age is, you can still do as you like. Ideally, Peggie would like to work in Child Services, bringing her drive and compassion to help the children who have been treated badly, to let those children know that they, too, can follow their dreams. "Treating them as through they don't care about them…" Peggie said to me, with her brow furrowing in frustration, "it's not fair for a little baby to have to be in a position like that."

The essay Peggie chose to contribute, *It is Never Too Late*, was the first essay that Peggie ever wrote – something she now sees as surprising. As Peggie explained, what she learns in her English class is knowledge she thinks she should have had a long time ago; but then, Peggie admits to having been more of a "math person" in high school. Furthermore, Peggie confessed to me that she received very little encouragement from her family in regards to her education; when Peggie became pregnant and had to drop out, she was actively dissuaded from returning back to school.

Yet, Peggie is not bitter about this. Those were different times, she says, when having a home and a family was considered more important for a woman than a diploma. Besides, as Peggie sees it, she has experienced and learned a lot in life since she was a teenage drop-out. Her priorities have changed. "You know, the goals that I have set for myself now, I didn't have back then…and right now, I don't feel it's too late to accomplish any of it."

At the closing ceremonies for the May-to-June cycle, Peggie would later seek to spread this message to all of her fellow learners. On the final day of each cycle, a brief, only somewhat formal gathering is held in order to give learners information for the upcoming cycle, as well as review the previous cycle. A number of learners advance to new reading or math levels at this time, and these men and women are recognized with certificates and applause. At the end of the announcements, learners are given the opportunity to stand up and speak. Honored as one of the students who would be advancing to the next level in both math and reading, Peggie asked to say a few words to the collected learners. As she thanked all of her teachers (especially Ms. Baxter), I could see the hope shine in her face; she was that much closer to achieving her goal. At the end Peggie used her own successes as an example to all. Echoing the rhetoric of her essay, she proclaimed "If I can do this, it's not too late for anyone else!"

We would all do well to listen to her.

It is Never Too Late by Peggie Gilmore

No matter where you live, it is never too late to set goals and follow your dreams. If you really want to do things for yourself, you have to do some footwork. You have to do research and open your mind to ideas. You also have to ask questions and make calls.

When I realized that it was not too late, I began to read different flyers about different schools, and which one would help me the most. The schools that I did research on, and called about were Harbor Campus, BCCC Liberty Campus, The Ripken Center, and The Learning Bank. After doing my footwork and research, I chose The Learning Bank.

If there is anyone out there that thinks it is too late, I suggest that you sit down and take a good look back over your life. I am glad that I chose The Learning Bank because it was what I was looking for. I truly enjoy going to the Learning Bank, because it is in my area. I like the teachers and the way they teach. I can understand the lessons that are taught. And most of all, I know that I can be successful, accomplish my goals, and make my dreams come true. And so can you; don't give up. If you have dreams and goals, then go for them – you can do it.

Leon Lovess, Sr.

My first interview for this project was Leon Lovess, an older gentleman who had been attending reading and writing classes at The Learning Bank for about a year. I was nervous, I admit – my hand shook a bit as a jotted down notes about his stories. I suppose that Leon sensed my nervousness, because when I began to ask questions, he used the universal tactic for getting someone to relax: he cracked a joke. In response to my question about his age, Leon replied to me: "Older than dirt. I was sitting at the right hand of God when he created the world, and he said 'Leon, turn on the light.'"

What else could I do, but laugh? The proverbial ice now broken, we began to talk in earnest. I could soon tell that the wit and whimsicality of that story are typical of Leon's very active imagination; an imagination which he insisted has been working fluidly since he was a child. Yet, it is only recently that Leon found an outlet for his creativity, and that is in writing. Writing which he had no confidence in until he decided to go for his GED.

According to Leon, the value of an education was never lost on him. Raised in a large family, where parents, siblings, uncles, aunts, and grandparents lived all lived under one, three-story roof, Leon recalls how his grandmother and great-uncle pushed him to become "an educated man" – "You better grow up to be something," they would say. However, as the eighth child out of nine, Leon has few memories of most of his older family members – that same grandmother and great-uncle died before Leon reached his teens, and even his oldest brother was in the army and moved out by the time Leon was grown-up enough to miss him. Still, his family always encouraged him, and spoke positively of the benefits of getting an education. Leon notes that this was especially true in the late 1940's and early 1950's, when to be educated as a young black man was difficult, but worthwhile.

Though Leon did not finish high school as we know it (instead, he entered a vocational school), he says that his brain has always "hungered for knowledge." He loved history and geography as subjects; today, most of his personal reading consists of articles about Black inventors, or African-American history. Since returning to his formal education, Leon has taken to writing short pieces of prose on the side: usually brief stories, like *The Pie Wars*, or character sketches such as *Billy Scott Washington*. Leon's interest in history has had a clear influence on pieces such as *Billy Scott Washington*, which is grounded in the history of Black culture just after the Civil War, while in contrast, a story like *The Pie Wars* draws on his more personal history, as he recalls starting food fights in school as a young child.

Leon takes great pride in his these stories, which, in turn, ultimately motivates his continuing education. As Leon explains, when talking about how education feeds his stories: "If I could spell, I could write anything." Pointing to my own handwriting as I took notes, Leon noted the speed and confidence that he percieved I wrote with; a surprise to me, since I thought my shaking hand was proclaiming my nerves to all in sight. And yet, it was that handwriting, that vocabulary which he envied.

Leon cites more than just what he's learned in school as inspiration; his religious upbringing has been a major influence on his writing and storytelling, especially with a short piece like *Angels on Earth*. The source of that story, Leon explained to me, came on a day when he noticed a neighbor of his giving food to people out on the street through a window in his house. "You don't see too many people that do things like that," Leon said; he then wrote *Angels*, which draws on a number of stories he has read about real people in newspaper articles.

Leon plans to keep writing with the encouragement of teachers, and his own children (who are college graduates, themselves) – after all, he hasn't yet run out of ideas. He'll learn as much as he needs to, for as long as it takes; writing means that much to him. Leon smiles when he talks about it, and when he says that his son once told Leon that one day his stories could be published. It looks like Leon is about to prove his son right.

Angels on Earth by Leon Lovess, Sr.

In every person there is goodness. We were not born with hate in our hearts. People who go out of their way to help someone without asking for money or rewards do it out of the goodness of their heart. I call them angels.

Example. In New York a grandmother who takes care of drug sick babies.

Example. A grandmother in California who feeds the homeless people out of her house.

Example. In a little town in Texas a grandmother who lived five miles from a prison. A prisoner, a three-time murderer, escaped and ended up at her house. He was a six-foot-seven, two hundred and fifty-pound man. She gave him something to eat. She prayed with him. She told him to go back: "God is with you."

A News reporter asked her, "Were you afraid?"

"No," she said, "God is with me."

The Pie Wars by Leon Lovess, Sr.

Bob and Ray were very good friends. On the Fourth of July, 2004, Ray gave a cookout in his backyard. Ray was putting food on the table when he slipped and a pie hit Bob in the face. Friends and family laughed at him. Ray smiled, and said, "Don't be mad, Bob."

Bob said, "You know this means war."

War, even in church and in stores and on the street. In the lunchroom. Even at the movies. One time at the car wash the pig was flying. Even at the wedding of one of their friends. Even family members got hit with pies. It was getting messy. It didn't stop there.

One time, Ray gets Bob when he was sleeping. Then, Bob and Ray's parents said: "This must stop, now."

But it didn't stop, for it went on for two months longer.

Billy Scott Washington by Leon Lovess, Sr.

Billy Scott Washington's parents were slaves in South Carolina. He worked alongside his mother and father as sharecroppers on the plantation. Billy had to work on other farms, and plantations to earn money. He saved up three hundred dollars.

His parents told him to go away and find a better life. Billy was sad to leave his parents. So he went west to Texas, to a little town called Dime Bank. Dime Bank was a mining town filled with outlaws and murderers. But five miles southwest of town there was a bigger town called Cold Water, which had a bank. One night, Billy was sitting in the back of the bar talking to a sickly old man named Jessie.

Jessie said, "I am old and dying. I have a mine. It's called the Fifty Dollar Mine. I want to sell it."

Billy said, "I'll buy it, how much?"

Jessie said, "I worked that mine for ten years and all I got was fifty dollars a month. That's why it's called the Fifty Dollar Mine."

Billy said, "I'll buy it."

Jessie said, "Sold." Billy gave him two hundred dollars. Jessie told him the mine was three miles northwest of town. "It is a hole in the side of the mountain," Jessie said.

Billy worked the mine for two years for fifty dollars a month. Jessie was right. But Billy worked hard day and night.

Then he hit a big vein of gold. He looked surprised, saying "The people in town can't know about this. They will kill me." Billy bought two mules and a wagon. He deposited thousands of dollars into the bank in Cold Water. Every time Billy came to town, the people laughed at him and called him "Fifty Dollar Mine."

The government bought Billy's mine for one million dollars. Billy went back to South Carolina and bought some land for him and his mother and father to live on. They had grown so old. Billy was fifty seven when he came home.

Althea Moore

"I shouldn't even be sitting here." It was that blunt, focused statement which began my interview with Althea Moore. She is a tall, intimidating woman; I would usually see her come to her evening classes at The Learning Bank dressed in scrubs, coming directly from her job as a medical assistant. Tonight, however, she is in clean-cut, professional clothes. She entered The Learning Bank a month ago – though she was unsure of the time frame, for "time goes kind of fast when you are preoccupied with studies." Althea is already just one level away from GED testing, and it seems as though she is poised to complete the program quickly, and move on to bigger things – perhaps, she has suggested, nursing school.

Yet, Althea does not see The Learning Bank as a mere means to an end. When she continued her opening statement, Althea explained to me that "I'm here for me…to become a whole person like I need to be. I don't want baggage in my life… [And] you can never know where you can go in life if you let fear and baggage stop you." Althea speaks in long, fluid sentences; she reminds me of a preacher who speaks with total conviction in her gospel truth – that education, that the act of reading, is essential to the person, and not just for money, a job, or career. It can help those, certainly, for as Althea has observed, "There's so many doors we don't know anything about…" without being able to read and write. Yet, the essential, core reason for doing this, to Althea, is "I can't function without it [my education]."

I asked Althea, then, why she felt it was so hard for other people to return to their education, if she believed it to be so very necessary. "I think…part of why some people don't go back [is] the frustration that they feel…" Althea has noticed that there is a certain attitude needed to take education seriously, one which only comes at a "different level in life, when you can no longer pretend like this isn't important." Yet, she also knows, from personal experience, that by the time you reach that age, the age itself is often a deterrent, and it can take a lot to realize that: "it's not about age or anything else."

Althea then started to tell me about her family; her older brother went to nearby Morgan State, and her sister entered the armed services. Althea was the only one who didn't complete high school. At the time, Althea found the curriculum repetitive, boring. Without more to stimulate her, she lost interest; something her family tried to prevent from happening. "I grew up in a home where education was important, but I was immature in my thought process about it." Althea told me that her brother, in particular, always believed that she could do "great things," but was afraid that once Althea left, she would never return to school.

Well, Althea matured, and years later, has found herself ready to swallow her fear, her "baggage" and pursue that GED. "I am trying to place myself in a certain position where I am comfortable, motivated to get education, and to have a better life...I want to say: 'I did this.'" Part of this maturing was raising her children – like many of the mothers here, at The Learning Bank, Althea refused to see her children succumb to the same flippancy she did. This was especially true of Althea's daughter, who she "pushed through high school. She [the daughter] almost didn't graduate." Ultimately, Althea had to confess to her own lack of a diploma in order to keep her daughter in school, and prove that Althea know what she was talking about. The news, said Althea, shocked her daughter, who had never known that her mother didn't graduate high school.

Yet, even as Althea's daughter graduated, Althea

knew she would have to return and get her GED,
to prove how truly important it is. "I didn't want to
continue to be a bad example. I have a decent job, and I
live a decent life, but I needed that education."

In coming to The Learning Bank, Althea found a
passion for learning which she hardly knew she had. It
seems that, when it came to scholarship, Althea "just
needed a little renewing." There are times when she is
certainly discouraged in class; "I am frustrated to others
around me not care as much." On the whole, however,
Althea likes the atmosphere, the small classes which
allow her the personal attention she used to get from
her older sister in her youth. Moreover, Althea began to
remember the good things she learned in high school,
things which had long been buried.

Althea especially remembers how teachers told
her she was "very intelligent, and information would
just flow out of me." Althea also had a very active
imagination, and her English teachers often encouraged
her to write. "Reading had been my friend," Althea
mused, remembering that "I would be punished at
home by being sent to my room, but I always read,
so it wasn't a real punishment." Yet, even as Althea
remembers all that she does know, she is more aware
of what she doesn't; Althea hopes to take computer
classes, recognizing how necessary computer literacy
is in today's world. Then, perhaps, Althea could take a
college course on writing, to follow in the footsteps of
the authors she admires – such as, and especially, Maya
Angelou.

Indeed, Althea had had the great honor of meeting
Maya Angelou some years ago, when the author was
performing a reading at a New Jersey church. Althea
made her way up to New Jersey just to see her – and
with great admiration, recalled how the poetess spoke
at length about her life, her background, and her

inspiration for her poems and books. When I asked Althea if she had ever written poetry, she shook her head. Poetry is still somewhat beyond her, since Althea doesn't feel as though she has the vocabulary to make them "jump off the page." Instead, Althea spoke with pride of a daughter who writes poetry; "I am fascinated that she can say so much, with so little."

Surely, Althea has just started to dream. She even said to me, eagerly: "Wouldn't it be fabulous if I saw my name on a book cover?" By pushing forward, with all her determination, Althea knows that anything is possible.

LaSharon Diggs

I met LaSharon Diggs during the first week I was at The Learning Bank, announcing the project and taking names of interested parties. LaSharon had not given me her name in class – rather, she approached me right as it was dismissed. She spoke to me shyly, quietly, about her "love poems," and asked if they were "okay" for the project.

So LaSharon and I sat down, and began to talk about poetry, and writing, and what it all meant to her. LaSharon first started writing poetry a decade ago, when her sister passed away in 1997. Her poems are fueled by what she feels when she is writing; as LaSharon explains it: "It's what I'm feeling at the moment. I learned that writing what I feel, I can express it better, because I'm so shy and emotional, so it comes out better on paper." Emotions – compassion, love, kindness, sorrow, and mourning – are all central to LaSharon's writing. She uses her poetry to channel what she otherwise says would be difficult for her to express.

Though LaSharon began writing poetry in her grief, when questioned as to her primary inspiration, the answer is an immediate "love." Certainly, it is plain that love is the source of LaSharon's two poems in this collection: titled *My True Love,* and *How Well Do You Know,* the poems talk about LaSharon's longtime boyfriend, Daymon. These were her first two poems of a total four which have been written to him – the latter of which, LaSharon shyly admits, was written while Daymon was with a different girlfriend. Once again, she chose poetry to reveal feelings which she otherwise would not have had the courage to express.

Now, however, LaSharon and Daymon have been dating for some time, and he is a constant source of support for LaSharon as she continues on with her education. Daymon will even call LaSharon on his breaks at work, which coincides with when the evening classes at The Learning Bank end.

LaSharon's enrollment in The Learning Bank came about when, after twenty-three years working as a geriatric nursing assistant, LaSharon decided she wanted to push herself farther in life: "someday I want to become an RN – a registered nurse. In order to, I've got to get my GED, so that I can go to college and earn my degree in nursing." So LaSharon started attending classes at The Learning Bank a year ago, in hopes of being able to further her career.

Yet, The Learning Bank has given her more than she anticipated – beyond her career hopes, LaSharon has found that she loves to simply *learn*. Of the environment at The Learning Bank, LaSharon says her favorite part is: "Learning…and listening is very important. And I learn…because even in general conversation we learn here; either your teacher is correcting your pronunciation, [or] sometimes they even give you vocabulary words. So it's just a learning experience here." LaSharon has also used her expanding vocabulary to her advantage in writing, finding better, and more varied words to use in her brief stanzas.

Since LaSharon's return to her studies, she has also started reading more frequently. Her tastes in novels reflect an interest in the "drama" of life; LaSharon reads everything from books about poverty, to crime, romance. She is naturally drawn to the heightened emotions of these stories. LaSharon has also read some poetry, but mostly experiments with different forms on her own, when it comes to writing.

Indeed, the forms LaSharon says she struggles with the most are rhyme schemes. "I try to stick with a rhyme scheme, but, if I can't put a word there that rhymes with the prior sentence, then I put what I feel." In the end, even form is subordinated all to LaSharon's truest feelings.

My True Love by LaSharon Diggs

My true love, knowing that
we had been there before makes
it so much better, because it's
true love we adore.
I always love you for sure.
I never felt secured until
you came back for what is yours.
I waited so long, you see, God
has his call. He made me to become
a woman with dignity and respect
to hold my own. He said, "trust
in thee," and I'll keep you strong.
I will send you your true love
and it won't be long. So I thank
he, to send me you (my true love)
with prayers nothing can go wrong.

How Well Do You Know by LaSharon Diggs

How well do you know,
when you hear that voice
and it lifts your mood.
How well do you know,
when his presence appears
and there isn't a single touch,
but just the warmth filling
from his breath.
How well do you know,
when all you see is the future.
How well do you know when
true friends have growth and patience and that lasts
forever.
How well do you know,
when staring in his eyes,
   honesty and not lies
How well do you know?

Rosa Lee McCray

I first encountered Rosa Lee McCray back in
December; on a visit to The Learning Bank to see
the staff and teachers, Leroy Young (the Assistant
Director), introduced Rosa to me as "our resident
poetess." Mr. Young handed me a copy of her poem, *I
am a Strong Black Woman*, and I was immediately struck
by the passion of her voice emanating off the paper. So,
when summer came and I was seeking writers for this
book, I immediately tracked Rosa down.

In person, I found that Rosa is shy, and quiet,
though as she speaks the strength of her convictions
comes across as strongly as the voice of her poem. Rosa
has been at the Learning Bank taking classes for three
years; she first came to The Learning Bank after her
son began taking classes (and, Rosa told me with pride,
he graduated from The Learning Bank just last year). It
was the encouragement of her son which really pushed
Rosa to return to her education, yet Rosa's motivation
can also be found in her love for her family, and her
desire to care for them as best she can. "Well, I been out
of school so long, and you know when you have your
children and your grandchildren who want you to read
something but you're not able to do it... that kind of
got me back."

It was in her first reading class at The Learning
Bank that Rosa wrote *I am a Strong Black Woman*.
Encouraged by the teacher to write poem, Rose says
that she found the topic for her writing came easily to
her: "It's about having God in my life, and you know,
[how that] made it so much more better...I think God
led me to write it. I never thought I could do anything
like that...it seemed like all the words just come
pouring out." Rosa is very active in her faith and at her
parish, having taken Bible study classes for a number
of years, serving as an usher on Sundays, and cooking
for the people there. Rosa's deeply-felt spirituality,

learned from her grandmother, has inspired her words, and provided and unwavering source of strength throughout her life.

Rosa also finds strength in her children. As stated in *I am a Strong Black Woman,* she had eight children; unfortunately, only four of them live today. Yet, aside from her own sons and daughters, Rosa has also raised two nieces, and five grandchildren after her youngest daughter died. Rosa says of her children: "They are so much a part of my life, they really are. They kept me going..." She speaks with great pride of the two granddaughters she raised from the ages of two and three: the younger now graduating high school to go on to college, and the elder out in the world, taking care of herself. Their capability and confidence was, no doubt, learned from the example Rosa set, as she dedicated everything to see them live healthy, strong, daring lives.

It has not been easy for Rosa to care for so many, but she has learned a lot from her experiences: "When you're growing up in poverty, you just learn to be strong, you know, as you get older, because that teaches you a lot... [My struggles] gave me a lot of courage." It is no surprise, then, that Rosa's favorite book is *American Heroes,* a book of stories about people who have overcome such obstacles as drug addiction and poverty to make better lives for themselves.

Rosa's ultimate dream is to go to college and become a chef. She loves to cook, and considers it her first passion; she even says that her pastor wants to help her start a small catering business. Rosa knows that education what will lead her on the path to achieve this dream. As her best words of advice to her grandchildren state: "Education is the most important thing in the world. Stay in school, get your education, 'cause you probably don't think it's important now, but when you get older you'll find out it's very important, very important."

I am a Strong Black Woman by Rosa Lee McCray

I am mother of seven children, but death has taken
four of them – three girls and one boy.
But God left me with two girls and two boys.
I had a hard time but the Lord brought me through.
But I am still standing tall
I have to put God first because he has always been
there
For me. Life without God—I am lost
I don't know what tomorrow will bring but I can't
Worry about that now
I want to learn everything I can
But it is hard, but life is hard but God is still there
For me
But you know I am still standing tall
I am growing every day. I just want God to
Keep me long enough to do some of the
Things I want to do
I am not where I want to be, but thank God I am
Not where I used to be.
I am a Strong Black Woman standing tall.

I am Not Looking Back by Rosa Lee McCray

I don't want to look back on my life when I was
a child; I want to look ahead. I just want good things
out of life. I just want to sit back and see where God
brought me from. Sometimes it is not good to look back.
I know what I went through as a child. It makes me
strong to see what is going on in the world today. God
will lead me to where he wants me to be. I would like
to go to college one day. My kids and my husband are
my pride and my joy. I love all of them, but God has to
come first in my life. God is in the midst of everything
I do. It if was not for God, where would I be? I will just
be still and let him do his work.

Charles Murphy

At fifty-one years old, Charles Murphy is ready
to just take life as it comes; but he is not ready to stop
doing as he pleases. Charles has seen a great deal of
this world, beginning in his days as military brat, when
he traveled across the country – from Washington,
the Kentucky, to South Carolina – and to different
countries such as Germany. The traveling of Charles's
childhood exposed him to a variety of cultures: music
especially, which would become Charles's greatest
passion. Yet, inherent in the youth of a military officer's
son is strict discipline; and Charles's step-father was no
exception in the rigid rules he imposed on Charles and
his siblings.

It was this very discipline which Charles says
profoundly (and negatively) affected his perception
of school: "You know, I had to shine boots, and clean
medals and stuff, and make sure the uniform was
straightened out; and I had other jobs around the house,
as far as cutting the grass, taking out the trash, washing
dishes and clothes and stuff like that." Perfection and
precision was expected of Charles in these tasks, and
the same standard was applied in his scholarly pursuits:
"And I went to school everyday, and when I went home,
I figured I did the best I could; but when I got home and
had homework, I had to deal with my father, and every
time I made a mistake I started getting buttwhipped.
So I'd just sit there and said 'the heck with it' and I just
quit trying."

When Charles entered adolescence, his initial
apathy evolved into active rebellion. Instead of
applying himself, Charles decided to just do as pleased
during school hours, and became a self-pronounced
"hustler." Soon, Charles's average school day contained
little actual class time: "After first period I had shop
class, and after that it was lunch, shooting dice, making

money, get a shot of wine underneath some trees, then go to music class. I had three lunch periods – I took them. I had one scheduled period and then I had two others." Charles wasn't alone in his escapades: his constant partner in crime during these days was an older brother, Urias, to whom Charles's brief letter, *Love for a Brother*, is dedicated.

"Me and Urias…they said we were [like] twins… [and] we always did things together. We stole donuts together, we was always skating together, rode bikes together…" The connection between Charles and Urias was special; for their mother had two husbands, and it was her first husband who fathered Urias and Charles, making Urias Charles's only full-blodded brother. Urias passed away about six years ago, as *Love for a Brother* mentions, but Charles still misses him greatly. "I guess we shared something that the rest of the kids in the family didn't share… we're Murphys."

Their mother's second husband was the military officer who ended up raising Urias and Charles, becoming "the only father I knew." Despite Charles's initial rebellion against his stepfather, he now acknowledges the long-term benefits of his childhood: "even though he [the stepfather] was a little tough on me, I figure he made me a better man, because you know he got me to the point where I have better morals and stuff…I can stick up for myself, now." Charles gives his step-father a lot of credit for instilling courage in him, and a real sense of what is right and wrong, even if it took until manhood for Charles to appreciate it.

Now, Charles wishes to reclaim his education, and learn what his indiscretions had distracted him from. Simply put, Charles returned to The Learning Bank because "I figured I was missing a lot by not being able to read." Lacking focus as an adolescent, Charles never quite mastered the skill; now, as an adult, he has the self-discipline, and desire to do so. In the poem *Only, Only, Only*, which was partially inspired by one of the first books Charles read for class, he describes literacy as a way to "grow." Although Charles is retired from working, he is not retired from living.

As Charles slowly gets back into the practice of reading, he has found that he enjoys books about musicians, especially rock and blues artists such as Jimi Hendrix and B.B. King – in this way, Charles has linked reading to his immense love of music, and that helps him continue to read.

Charles plays the lead guitar, and he admitted to me that he would be content to do nothing but play that during his retirement. At the closing ceremony for the June cycle this summer, Charles granted us all a chance to see him play. He seemed completely at home with a guitar in his hand; he easily played requests from the learners – older, bluesy rock songs that suited his deep, raspy, voice. I could clearly see what he meant when he said that he would be content to "sit at home and play my guitar and go to church, and travel around playing my guitar, and enjoy life and enjoy playing for the Lord," for the rest of his retirement.

Still, Charles sees his G.E.D. as a necessary experience in life, one to add to his already long list. "At least I'll know I've accomplished getting a GED or a diploma," Charles says, though he has yet to make any plans for after he has graduated. Of course, Charles doesn't need them right away; he can wait and see what he's called to do. In the meanwhile, Charles will simply relax, guitar in hand. Somewhere, Urias is probably listening, and tapping his foot along to the rhythm.

Love for a Brother by Charles Murphy

Hi. My name is Charles Murphy. I had a bother named Urias who passed away a few years ago. He was my best friend in the world. He stood five foot, three inches, small framed, thin, with a light brown complexion.

I always had a good time with him even when we got in trouble. Urias would coax me to do the wrong thing and we'd both get a butt wippin,' then laugh about it and curse under our breath. As we grew older, we drifted apart. He got into drugs, and so did I. He passed in late May of 2001, but he still lives in my heart.

P.S. I love you Urias
Charles

Only, Only, Only by Charles Murphy

Only as high as I reach can I grow;

I am reaching for my GED
and that is a part of growing
in knowledge.

Only as deep as I look can I see;

I have began looking into
programs that might help me
with my life ahead.

Only as much as I dream I can be;

I am dreaming not to have any
financial difficulties and live
a long a perspires life helping
others in need.

Arthur Thomas Goodin

It is two days before Arthur Thomas Goodin's (he is very precise in telling me to use his middle name) birthday when I have the chance to sit down and talk with him. He will turn sixty the day after tomorrow; but he's not making a big fuss about it. Arthur's days since he started attended The Learning Bank last summer have become fairly regular, rhythmical: "I just want my GED, you know…that's why I come to the Learning Bank everyday that I can…[I] go to work, try to rush off the job and come here." For Arthur, The Learning Bank is the means to a cherished goal, and possibly the last goal he may be able to achieve in his lifetime.

Now, Arthur has spent most of his life in Baltimore; he moved here in early adulthood with a girlfriend and their oldest child. In his time as a Baltimore resident, Arthur has experienced a lot of the city's growth: he worked on many distinguished building projects, including Camden Yards, M&T Bank Stadium, Johns Hopkins University, and the Johns Hopkins Hospital. He has laid pipe under our roads, and logged trees for our wood. Yet, for as much as Arthur has contributed to Baltimore, it was his childhood in a small, rural suburb of George Town, South Carolina that Arthur decided to write about in his essay, *Working My Way Up*.

"It was a little town," Arthur says, as he describes his birthplace and adds details to what he wrote in the essay, "out on the outside of Georgetown, South Carolina. And when you get out of the city limits, so far down, there's a little town called Midway." According to Arthur, his family just about dominated several blocks of land in Midway – some of whom, including one of Arthur's six sisters, still live in the area. Midway has become somewhat modernized, now; a small airport was built in the area, now mostly used by private planes. Yet,

Arthur can recall a time when he, his mother, and his thirteen siblings had no gas, no electric, and no phone: costing ten dollars a month, it wasn't until Arthur was nine years old and able to work odd jobs himself that the family could afford it.

Since he was able to, Arthur has been working – and this means for most of his life. He has done everything from working on green tobacco farms in North Carolina, to the aforementioned logging, to loading up large, flatbed trucks with wood for his uncle, for fifty cents – money which was always given directly to his mother. As seen in Arthur's essay, his mother worked long hours, too – and this was done despite suffering from what Arthur describes as "bad nerves." After working all day, and babysitting at night, Arthur's mother would then work diligently by the firelight to sew clothes for her children.

Such circumstances made attending school regularly quite difficult, especially for the boys. Arthur told me: "I've got six brothers, and five living, and none of the boys got their high school diplomas; but all of my sisters, except the one who died, all of them went to college and got their high school diplomas." The boys, it seems, had to work especially hard; yet their work paid in off in being able to afford to buy books for their sisters. Though there was a public education system, when Arthur was a child it was still segregated; as a result, under funded black schools, especially in rural areas, often had to charge their students for books. As Arthur describes it: "In the black schools, we had to pay for books...they didn't give us no free books like they got the opportunity to today, they didn't have it, at least not back then. And they would let us read, share, and borrow books... but they couldn't do it all the time 'cause they'd run out of books and stuff like that..."

The struggle to afford school materials, plus the

burden of working, meant that Arthur was in and out of school until he was eighteen – at which point he had only passed as far as the seventh grade level. At eighteen, Arthur decided to quit school permanently; shortly after, he moved to North Carolina, and then later settled in Baltimore. Yet Arthur never entirely gave up his mission to achieve an education; "when I got out, I start reading the billboards and learning how to spell those small words, and sometimes I get to a big word and learn how to spell that, too... And when I used to get the chance I would, you know, read anything I could read and stuff like that. I wasn't good at spelling but I always could read, you know, read words that I can't spell."

Of this adjustment from rural South Carolina to urban Baltimore, Arthur says: "City life is...it ain't that easy, you know...I got hooked up with the wrong crowd, you know, by the end. And I got into fights and stuff like that, and I went to jail but, just to protect myself, that's all I was fighting about, protecting myself." Eventually, Arthur's behavior led him to a program called Total Healthcare; they referred him to The Learning Bank.

For Arthur, coming to The Learning Bank was an entirely new experience for him. Where school had made Arthur feel discouraged before, he now felt supported: "And when I come here, I told Ms. Butler [the head of the Evening Program] things that I can't do. But Ms. Butler, she built my hopes up, you know, and tell me I can do it, you know...she give me confidence, says 'you can do it.' And I've learned a whole lot since I've come here to the Learning Bank... that's something you got to tell somebody, they're doing good, and if they ain't doing real good, still say that they're doing good, build their hopes up to where they can do better, whether it's a child or a grown person."

Arthur views earning his GED as one of his last, great goals in life: "this is something I got to do, that I want to do. This is my goal right now, for me to meet, and if I don't get a chance to meet no more goals, I'm still gonna be working on this one…This is, like, the thing I had to do, coming up." Arthur only wishes that everyone else could appreciate opportunity as much as he does: "I mean, like those kids on the corner, we need someone to talk to them… there's plenty of opportunity out here to go to school, see, if you don't know something You'd be surprised people out there on the street don't pay no attention to this…"

Now, Arthur is immensely proud of how far he has come in the years since he first learned to sign his name and write out his social security number. "Now I ain't bragging on myself, but for to me read as good as I do right now since I come to the Learning Bank, I think it's good." In two days, when Arthur turns sixty, he will be sitting for his GED. That last goal is just in sight.

Working My Way Up by Arthur Thomas Goodin

My name is Arthur T. Goodin, born in the suburb of George Town, S.C., in a little place called Midway. I lived in a two bedroom house, with thirteen brothers and sisters.

My mother worked two jobs, day and night. She cleaned house in the daytime from 8 a.m. to 6 p.m., came home, and went back to work at 7 p.m. til 12 or 1 a.m. babysitting. So we, my brother and sisters, watched each other. Sometimes I had to stay home and take care of my little sisters.

My father died, so my mother had to make my sisters' school dresses. We had wood heat. So the boys had to keep firewood in the house until my mother went to bed at 3 a.m. in the morning. My mother couldn't pay for all of us school book. Sometime I had to read from the girl or boy next to me.

When I was ten years old, my older sister left South Carolina, and went to North Carolina, and worked with green tobacco. It was a hard time!

Now I'll be sitting on June 14 for my GED. I am going for my gold: getting my GED so I can have bigger and better things!

♦ Conversion
From Object to Subject

How do you conceive of yourself, as an individual?

This is not an easy question to answer – it brings in many, many other questions. It is nearly impossible for us to have any sense of who we are without surroundings – without an environment of people and things to which we compare ourselves. Our concept of "self" is created by drawing boundaries between "me" and "not me." Jean-Paul Sartre has rather accurately observed: "I need the Other in order to fully realize all the structures of my being."[1]

Indeed, one of the most popular theories about self-concept in sociology today reflects that view: a contemporary of Sartre's, Eviatar Zerubavel, proposes a similar theory in his essay, *Islands of Meaning*. Zerubavel describes the ideas and connections of the human mind like tiny islands, where similar ideas are grouped together, but dissimilar ones are separated by wide stretches of the river *different* – and so it is the differences which create boundaries keeping Me in, and Them out. These boundaries may be natural ones, giant mountains and rivers imbedded in our mind by societal standards. Or, they could be individually tailored fences and canals, carefully erected in our minds through personal needs and experience.

In this sense, we sit on the shores of our islands of Self, and stare suspiciously across at the nearby island of Them. Self will never entirely trust *Them*. Them can be composed of ideas which threaten our normality, our accepted reality. Self does not usually like to challenge the status quo: to quote a line from the musical *1776*, "Men with nothing would usually rather prefer the *prospect* of becoming rich, than face the reality of being poor." Oh, we hear about the great war of Us verses Them, but the real war is really the Self verses Them, for it is Selves, similar selves, which compose the Us, and which fight ruthlessly to protect what they believe is the right, the true, the genuine.

But then, there are traitors to Us among the Selves. There are Selves who look across at other islands and see something which affects them, something which appeals to them. Those Selves take these new ideas; they study them, learn about them, and internalize them. Then, the geography of their island starts to changes, the boundaries formed by association shift – Self changes because its Them has become something else, something once accepted as true, but no longer.

This action, then, is conversion. Conversion, though a word usually associated to religion, isn't limited as thus. Rather, conversion, a "turning" of the self "against" something according to the Oxford English Dictionary, can be said to exist wherever an individual has changed the foundation their sense of Self was built on, and begin to change their former assumptions about good and bad, right and wrong, true and false, Self and Them.

In my time at The Learning Bank, I encountered many individuals who spoke of "conversions," religious or otherwise. It was an unfortunately common story to hear learners speak about recovering from drug addiction, leaving gangs, and other such destructive behaviors; and all of these learners held their education to be the essential tool for leaving the structures of their former selves behind. Five of those stories appear here: Bern Davis, Beverly Jackson-Zen, Shannon

Baytops, Anthony Brown, and Charles Vessells. Each
of their conversion stories is unique – some speak
of incarceration, some speak of church, and some of
loving and patient family members who constantly
urged them to leave islands of drug addiction and pain
and find a place of health and happiness.

The attitude which each of the learners takes
towards their conversions is also unique, each just a
little different from the next. There is Bern, who in
titling his piece *A Negative History* betrays the guilt
and sorrow he still feels about past decisions. There
is Beverly, who believes in her salvation as a miracle
of Christ's power. She regrets her past as one regrets
sin – though she believes herself to be forgiven, she
still shakes her head and clucks gently at a mislead
youth. Shannon is similar to Beverly, in that her faith
has helped come so far; but she has also drawn on her
strength as a mother, and the love of her children to
change her life around. Anthony faces his story with
stoic honesty – he did what he did, and nothing will
ever change that. Finally, there is Charles – Charles
who, as his essay indicates, appreciates his past; the
past has made him stronger. Yet all of these different
individuals converge on the same point: a change was
needed. Conversion happened. None of them claim it
was easy, but it was necessary.

The great common thread between all four stories
– or "witnesses," as some call it, is a desire to do exactly
that: witness to the world about their struggles, their
pain, their sorrow, all in the hopes of helping someone
else who faces the difficulties they did. Coming out of
their experiences, Bern, Beverly, Shannon, Anthony,
and Charles all know that there is more than drugs, the
street, or incarceration; they know that men and women
are meant to be more. Prometheus, perhaps, saw in
humanity that same potential, one which only needed a

proverbial spark to ignite it.

Humanity's potential is what Paulo Freire calls the "ontological vocation" of all humankind to be Subjects: self-aware, self-possessed, self-controlled beings whose fate is not at the whim of an addiction, or jailer. What's more, they want to help others reach that realization, too; to move from being objects that are acted upon, to subjects who act. This conversion is not unlike the release from Plato's cave, through passages lit by Prometheus's torch. It is a full realization of the possibilities contained within an individual, which education brings to the forefront.

In this sense, Bern, Beverly, Shannon, Anthony, and Charles are writing their words to "convert" the world, another essential action to Freire's philosophy of subjectivity. "To speak a true word," writes Freire, "is to transform the world." The truth of the witness given by these men and women furthers their subjectivity and liberation – for the truest mark of a Subject is to act to affect the reality around him or her. Not only are these learners reflecting on their earlier position as objects, they are also calling others to recognize their objectification, using their words to promote action. Anthony's ending phrase, "Never pick up drugs. Drugs are for losers," is a particular example of how he sees his "testimony" – more than a story, it is meant to appeal to those who have had similar experiences, and warn those who may stray. Shannon also reflects this – she has used, and hopes to use, the story of her past as a tool to save other troubled youth. And Beverly witnesses to the world about her conversion – because God called her to do so, to bring faith to others.

However, the words of these learners are not for the oppressed, alone. To everyone, whether you are Christian or not, have struggled with addiction, or not, been incarcerated, or not, these are powerful stories of hope. Even in the direst circumstances, even after years of abuse to the mind, body, and soul, there is redemption. Like the men and women in the previous chapter, Bern, Beverly, Shannon, Anthony, and Charles knew that it wasn't too late to transform their Selves; and then, the world around them.

Bern Davis

"A change in life, trying to better my life." Such is Bern Davis's simple reason for the pursuit of a G.E.D. Bern is in his late thirties, and he speaks to me with a deep, rough, gravelly voice which sounds ages older that he is. Bern tells me that he has only been at The Learning Bank for three months; yet, Bern says it took twenty years to get here, in such a way that I wonder if it is an insightful joke, or a joking insight.

Bern made the choice to drop out of school in the ninth grade, and it is one that he still regrets, which he believes defined his past, casting it in a negative light – hence the title of his essay, *A Negative History*. Bern really did enjoy learning when he was younger, for as he explains, "I enjoyed when I went, and I was never no fool. I just got sidetracked by foolish pleasure." Bern recalls how he particularly enjoyed math: "There's like, tricks to math – if you just catch the little trick to it, you'll catch right onto it." Throughout his youth, Bern was encouraged by his older sister, who he remembers as being quite intelligent. Before high school, Bern would often go to her for help, learning those mathematical tips and tricks under her tutelage. That is, until Bern came into ninth grade, and the whole atmosphere of school seemed to change for him: "I got bored after reaching the ninth grade…it seemed like we were being taught the same thing over, and that made it boring, but I didn't know they was pushing this in your head…" Bern adds, after a thoughtful moment's pause, "I notice this now."

It was in that first year of high school that Bern became involved in drugs, and right as he was ready to pass on to the tenth grade, Bern dropped out. As Bern phrases it: "I never was no fool, but I just made the unwise choice of quitting school." In *A Negative History*, Bern confesses to his decades-long cycle of using, and the hurt he caused to his family. Then, merely nine months ago, Bern decided to change his life around. He realized that he needed to stop hurting those who loved him the most. So he entered a recovery process to shed his addiction and improve his life.

In the course of Bern's recovery, he remembered the importance of his education: "I got into the recovery process, and everybody else I was watching anticipated getting jobs. And I looked, and remembered how important education was; you can get a better job with your education." Still, the decision to return to school was not an easy one for Bern to make; at thirty-eight years old, Bern couldn't imagine that there was anyone as old as he was going for a basic G.E.D. This, Bern realized, was a complete "misunderstanding."

Bern describes his first few experiences at The Learning Bank with a smile: "What really caught my attention, and made me not as nervous as I was, was the Learner's Bill of Rights up there on the board..." On the main level of The Learning Bank, there is a large bulletin board, decorated with bright colors, and right in the center there is a plain piece of white computer paper, on which is printed this "Bill of Rights" – conceived and written by The Learning Bank staff. "...[The Learner's Bill of Rights] really gave me an understanding, and made me comfortable, because I was a little nervous to be thirty-eight years old and coming back to get your GED. And I read that, and it sort of helped me a lot." Once Bern relaxed in his new learning environment, he started to plan his future, possibly going on to college so that he could work with at-risk youth - like he was once - as a counselor.

As for his *Negative History*, Bern hopes that it will make an impact on that very same audience: "Because I was born and raised in these types of neighborhoods, and I look at these young guys and I feel like and somebody that made the same mistake they're making right now could probably help them... explain to them what I've been through and help [them] avoid making the same mistakes that I did." No one, believes Bern, should have to deal with the hindrance that an incomplete education can be. "You might not feel it or see it not, but later on in life...It limits you from doing something later on that you might want to do." Bern hopes to never fall subject to those limits – self imposed, or imposed by others – again.

A Negative History by Bern Davis

I am writing this to have people understand that I am a better person. The reason I chose this subject is because for twenty years or more I lived my life under the influence of several mind-altering chemicals. I did this for so long, I became comfortable with it, not really minding the pain and destruction I was causing. My thinking and behavior were both dysfunctional. The only things that really mattered to me involved drugs: either using or dealing. I used to think I could deal without using. But in the end I started the same behavior of using and dealing all over again.

The reason I say I am a better person, is because I was a selfish person. So I am now in the recovery process, and it really helped to open my mind to a better understanding of myself. Since I was using, and only hung around people who used like myself, they were the only ones I would listen to. I thought when my family and friends who didn't use gave me good advice that they were being nosy, and didn't understand. My dysfunctional thinking didn't allow me to realize they were the ones that really cared.

Now, after being in the recovery process for nine months, I learned a number of things about myself; some good, some bad. I learned how overly sensitive I was. I used in the end of my active addiction because I didn't want to leave the people I became attached to. Plus, I was comfortable with the destructive way I was living.

But deep in my heart, I had this strong desire to get better. Then one day I took the needed steps to get my life together. Now after being in this new way of life for nine months, I have learned a number of things about myself. Not all of what I learned was good, but the bad that I experienced will help me not turn back.

Beverly Jackson-Zen

Sometimes, I've found that the best stories come to you when you aren't looking for them. And that is how I met Beverly Jackson-Zen.

One evening at The Learning Bank I was poking my head into classrooms, anxiously looking for a student who said she could meet with me that day who had yet to show, when Beverly walked up to me and asked: "Are you the one that's doing that poetry book?"

Caught somewhat off-guard, I smiled and answered yes, also adding that it wasn't exclusively poetry. To this, Beverly replied: "Well, I wasn't going to do it, but then I was just inspired by God, and he told me to write my testimony. So I did, and I'd like it to be in your book, please."

After a statement like that, I was eager to hear the story Beverly wished to share. So we went to the nearby library, and in the quiet there, Beverly gave me her testimony. Her faith spilled over into everything she said – in every topic, she found God, or she lamented the lack of God. Hence the title of her essay: *A Life With and Without Jesus.*

According to Beverly, she struggled in school; she was eventually classified a special needs student and placed in what she terms the "slow class." As a result, she received very little encouragement in school; because of Beverly's placement, her friends had given her up for a lost cause, and only her parents really pushed her to perform. By the time Beverly entered high school, she was without an in-school support system to keep her going. Then she became pregnant with her daughter and dropped out of school entirely.

However, Beverly had a grandfather who never gave up hope and truly sought to instill in her the importance of education. "I promised my grandfather years ago – when I dropped out of the ninth and got pregnant. He told me 'Go back to school and finish your education, because you're going to need your education when you get older for a job, or just in life, period.'"

It would be a long time before Beverly could fulfill that promise. After dropping out of high school, Beverly struggled with alcoholism; yet even in this, she attributes God's watchful eye in preventing her from falling into harder drugs, as she has seen her husband do. However, it was in meeting her future husband that Beverly became connected to the drug recovery program associated with American Rescue Workers' Church – a meeting which she writes about in *A Life With and Without Jesus*. Although primarily meant for men, the American Rescue Workers' Church had a profound impact on Beverly's own use of alcohol, and the faith she found there helped her to give it up. Unfortunately, Beverly has watched her husband struggle with falling off the wagon over the years. Despite this, their marriage continues intact – because Beverly has put all her trust in God.

Finally, Beverly was able to follow through on her promise to her grandfather in March of 2007, when her younger sister (also a student at The Learning Bank) told her about the program, and convinced her to sign up. Beverly soon found that returning to finish her education could help in her faith-life. Beverly notes that in school she "didn't like reading too much. I couldn't read that good, but since I've been going to church, and reading the Bible and everything, God inspired me to stick with it, and now I know more, more than I did then, and I can read a lot better. Since I've been coming here, I can read pretty good." Beverly has also found the environment friendlier than her old DNC classes, implying that she felt rushed and overwhelmed in school when she says: "Here, if ...[the teachers] see that you need more time with certain, certain things, they stick with you until you get it, until you understand. And then they'll come back and make *sure* you understand." That willingness to let Beverly learn at her own pace is something she wishes she had had in her younger days.

In the past year, Beverly really feels as though she has come into her own in her faith; even finding her own church, outside of her husband's influence. As she works towards achieving her GED, Beverly hopes to use her education in ministry. "Share God even more," Beverly says, when I ask about her post-GED plans, "you know, I believe my gift from Him is to help people, to help people less fortunate than I am." And she has started, by sharing her testimony.

A Life With and Without Jesus by Beverly Jackson-Zen

When I was thirty years old, me and my daughter were living in a nice townhouse with my ex-boyfriend. I thought that living there without Jesus in my life or my daughter's life was okay. I thought Nicole and I were okay. But I was not truly happy with living in sin with my boyfriend; we were getting high and hanging out.

One day, Nicole and I were standing in front of Cross Street Market, ready to catch the bus to go up town, when a young guy, Steven, came up to us and asked where to buy some body oil. So, Nicole and I showed him the store. The guy was interested in me, and he asked me, "Do you know Jesus Christ as your Savior?"

I said, "A little bit." And he was telling me about Jesus Christ, and he invited Nicole and I to American Rescue Workers' Church, where he was staying.

So, we went there for church service, and Nicole and I ended up getting saved. Steven and I ended up getting married nine months later, and we've been together ever since for twelve long years, both good and bad.

But without God in our lives we wouldn't be together today, with his drinking and drugging, and my fooling around with other guys off and on. But we had God in and out of both our lives. Now, we both know we have to be on fire for the Lord. But if you are lukewarm, He will pour you out of His mouth. Amen.

Shannon Baytops

The first thing I noticed upon meeting Shannon Baytops, was how young she looked. Though thirty-eight years old, Shannon's eyes are large, dark, and shine with an indescribable innocence, a blend of shyness and eagerness which I don't often see in the faces of the adults at The Learning Bank; especially not in those of the evening program, who are often attending classes on top of working full time – and then some.

Yet, the air of youth and innocence in Shannon does not cover the careworn lines on her forehead, often wrinkled, I'm sure, in worry over her three children. Those three children whom, Shannon tells me, helped her turn her life around. "The one thing that I wish I could change the most from my past, is being on drugs, and being on drugs while pregnant with my daughter, and all the things that I went through: jail, losing custody of her, fighting to get her back..." Shannon's voice strained as she told me this – though she has written about such struggles in class, and shared them with many others through the years of her recovery, her remorse still pains her. Shannon's return to education at The Learning Bank is, more than anything else, a continued attempt to remove herself from that past. "I'm thirty-eight years old now, and I wanted my education and my diploma..." Shannon then bluntly described how she felt without that diploma: "I was empty inside without it. I did not like that."

So, in January of 2007, Shannon began taking classes for the first time since she was a teenager, and now she takes them much more seriously. The work is hard, Shannon told me, but she enjoys it – again, mentioning the essay she wrote about getting custody of her daughter. Assignments such as that have shown Shannon just how much she has grown. "When I was younger, I just didn't have the time [to write]. I thought drugs was the most important thing, and I went through a lot of experiences in my life, and I felt like that I wasn't grown up – growing up, and even after I came off the drugs, I still felt empty inside. It wasn't until I came and signed up for school that I knew I was complete..."

Seeing just how important Shannon's education has become for her, it is no surprise, then, that she sought to instill the same love of learning her children. Shannon was not about to let them lose focus the way she did in her youth. "I didn't have the support that I – that I had for my kids. I didn't have somebody who'd get me out of here, get me to school, tell me read your book, get your homework out. I didn't have that. I guess that's why I encourage my kids to go to school, to do their homework, and write their book reports, and do the essays and all of that."

Shannon smiled, a bit shyly, as she said that. The pride she has in her children was clear in each word, especially as she spoke of her two oldest, high school-aged children: "Seeing my son going across the stage in 2005, and my other daughter is about to come out, meant a lot to me." Shannon added that her son's graduation gave her extra motivation to achieve her own graduation. "I think that it encouraged me to go back because I've been so hard on them to finish school. How can I say to them that this is the right thing to do when I didn't do it? So I went back to show them that."

Indeed, Shannon has always taught by example. She has never hidden her past from her children, but uses it to teach a lesson which she doesn't want them to learn from experience. "I've always shared my experience [with my children], to the best of my abilities, and actually told them how I fell flat, went downhill after I dropped out, and explaining to them what drugs do to you and how the street whipped me..." Doing so for her children has led to Shannon's hopes of becoming a social worker for juveniles. She truly believes that it takes someone who has "been there" to reach out to the youth headed there: "So, I think for the most part in sharing that with a lot of teenagers...would help them out a great deal to stay in school and don't do drugs."

More than that, though, Shannon feels a real obligation to serve others; she is a "saved individual," and spoke of how she gives God all the credit for the good in her life. "I feel like God has taken of me for thirty-eight years, and through all the things that I have done in my life. I think that I deserve to give something back." Her language here, in particular, really struck me; "I deserve to give something back." To Shannon, service is not an obligation, not a way to redeem herself – no, her education is that – but a gift. The chance to help another person is a blessing, a blessing begun with the daughter who changed her life, which continues on today, and for as long as Shannon pursues her education – her dream.

Anthony Brown

Anthony Brown, a lanky man with wire-rimmed glasses, is absolutely determined to finish his education. He is forty-seven years old, and comes into The Learning Bank Monday, Tuesday, Wednesday, and Thursday of each week. Each day I see Anthony walk in for class, moving slowly because of a large black air-cast around one of his legs, while a stack of workbooks and notebooks are nestled in the crook of his left arm, and a red-knit lanyard weighed down with keys swings gently around his neck. On the day I am supposed to interview Anthony, he seeks me out, first; anxiously, he tells me his essay is unfinished, yet he is still eager to share his story with me.

"When I was going to finish [my essay]," Anthony starts off by telling me, "I was going to go ahead and give the kids advice to go to college...you know, don't make the mistakes that I made..." Anthony also tells me the title of his autobiographical essay, *The Life and True Testimony of a Drug Addict*; and surely, there is not a better word for the story he tells than "testimony." In his writing, Anthony lists out those "mistakes" of his, describing a pattern and cycle of drug use and incarceration which it took a true conversion for him to overcome. Yet, far from this being a simple acknowledgement of his past, the essay describes a hope for the future, a hope that Anthony has found in his faith, and in a Christian-based recovery program located in East Baltimore.

Indeed, it was Anthony's recovery process that caused him to come to The Learning Bank. As Anthony describes the process: "Part of the program was that you had to go to school. And I went to school, and I took the GED test, and I only failed by like, maybe fifteen points in three subjects. And that's the three subjects I'm coming back to take." Having now returned to the pursuit of his education, Anthony looks back on his past actions in school, and sees in himself a great deal of evolution. Once shy and quiet in the classroom, Anthony is now no longer afraid to speak up, participate in class, read out loud, and make his opinions known. In Anthony's own words: "I don't worry about what nobody think of me no more, as far as if I answer a question and it might be wrong or something like that... [and] I never did that in school." His teachers, Anthony says, rarely seemed to have extra time to dedicate to him – it wasn't that they didn't care, he explains, but that they "did what they had to do and moved on, that's all." It's clear that Anthony doesn't blame anyone but himself for dropping out; the teachers did their job as best they could, and Anthony was the one who failed to do his part.

At home, things weren't much different. Anthony admits that when he was younger, he was far too proud and far too concerned with his image to take the advice of his family, where his five sisters and parents constantly encouraged him to work harder in school. "I was the one they call the black sheep, the hardest head. I just wanted to do things my way." Obstinate as he was, Anthony ignored his family just as he often ignored teachers.

Today, however, Anthony will not accept that attitude from his own child, a fifteen-year-old girl in her first year of high school. "All I want her to do is give me that piece of paper," Anthony declares, referring to the diploma, "let me see [it]." To Anthony's mind, "That paper is a real important asset to put in your life, because without it it's hard to get a good job. And I drilled that in my daughter's head." Anthony hopes to persuade her to see what he never saw as a child: that an education is essential, not superfluous, and that life on the street is not as glamorous as it might seem.

As for Anthony's own plans, once he receives his GED, he hopes to find a job where he can work inside, away from the elements for a while. In the meanwhile, Anthony spends much of his time giving back to his community by doing service work with his parish: "[It's] just like, passing out food and stuff like that in the church. You got people who come out with vouchers and stuff like that, and you make bags of food and give it to them. Then I clean up in the church, cleaning bathrooms and sweeping...I just try to keep myself busy..." Anthony's desire to serve others seems to be part of why he agreed to speak to me; ultimately, Anthony hopes that people can learn from his testimony. He wants to provide an example to everyone: to prevent people from using drugs, and to show those who do use them that hope is there. "I changed my life around," Anthony says, "I gave my life to God, and people can change." There is no doubt that Anthony has come a long way; he will testify as much to anyone he meets.

The Life and True Testimony of a Drug Addict
by Anthony Brown

My full name is Anthony Brown, better known by the people as Rickey, standing five-foot-eight, weighing one-hundred and sixty-five pounds of bone and muscle. I am a forty-seven-year old black male, and have lived in Baltimore City all my life. I have five sisters and two brothers and I am the youngest boy in my family.

I started using drugs at the age of fourteen. I started hanging around the wrong crowd in junior high school, and was introduced to drinking wine, smoking weed, and popping pills. I think peer pressure had a lot to do with it, also. But anyways, this also lead to me getting myself in trouble with the police.

The first time I got arrested, I thought my mom was going to kill me. My first arrest was for robbing a guy coming out of a gas station. I will never forget that, because my homeboy – who was always my partner in crime – went to pull out his gun from his clip, and shot himself in the foot. That was so funny, I laughed so hard that I almost pissed on myself, and got myself caught.

We both did one year in the Maryland Training School. I got into a lot of fights in that place. When I came home, I started hanging around the wrong people again, but that was when I was introduced to selling dope, and having sex with older women. I was about fifteen and a half years old then, and I thought I was the coolest, slickest young guy in my neighborhood. I sold drugs until I was eighteen years old, and that's when I started using it myself. Doing dope is what I'm talking about. That was the biggest mistake I ever made in my life.

My life has not been the same since I took that first blast shot. My life has been going up and down, up and down for the last twenty-eight or twenty-nine years. I just could not seem to get it together, no matter how hard I tried. I have been in prison so many times I can't even count them. I have been homeless, sleeping on park benches, parked cars, vacant houses or wherever else I could sleep. There was something in my life that I was missing, and I just could not figure out what it was. Why couldn't I just have a normal life, and be a productive tax paying citizen? What was I doing wrong?

It took me almost thirty years to finally realize what it was, and that is God in my life. I gave my life to God six months ago, and my life has not been the same since. I don't do drugs anymore. I've been a free man for two years now: no probation or parole. I now live in my own apartment and I am back in school today trying to get my GED. God has turned my life around a whole 180 degrees. My Lord and Savior Jesus Christ is the best friend I ever had. I am going to end this essay now, but I hope and pray that whoever reads this will learn a little something from it.

Never pick up drugs.
Drugs are for losers!!!

Charles Vessells

"My name is Charles Vessells, v as in Victor, e-s-s-e-double-l-s." This is how Charles begins his interview, showing his detail-oriented personality. The precision marks the tone for the rest of the interview, as Charles explains to me his reasons for participating in the project.

Before I even ask a question, Charles has something important for me to know. "I am honored and privileged...and grateful, for the opportunity, and years left in my life to get a better perspective...I can't get back the past that I lost, but I can instill goals and aspirations in them." Charles speaks, referring to his daughter and two grandchildren. He is a short, wiry man with a hint of white in his dark, close-cropped beard; that salt-and-pepper look is one of the only indicators to his age: fifty-three years. It is quickly apparent just how much Charles has seen and learned in those years, and how much knowledge he can pass on to everyone around him. Yet, only recently did Charles's education become focused in the formal, academic sphere; as a child, he saw little value in the time he spent in a classroom:

"At the time, when I was in school, I didn't enjoy anything about it. That's why I didn't continue... because I was kinda misled about life, what was important, and some of the things dealing with being a productive individual and educating yourself." Continuing on with an honesty that displays the clarity of his hindsight, Charles admits that "I didn't know no better, to appreciate school....I kinda was influenced and misled about some of the things in society that I gave praise to...like the use of drugs, [or] trying to take from other people and not work for them, which landed me in prison numerous times."

In prison, Charles says he went into "survival mode," occasionally attending school there, but mostly just trying to make it through his sentence, and working the state-issued jobs. Yet Charles's incarceration did cause him to appreciate, just a bit more, the importance of literacy: "I did take more initiative to try to begin to read. I wasn't a great reader, but it helped passed the time." Moreover, Charles began to get a sense of something bigger than him: "I started reading the newspapers, magazines, and recognizing that there was more to life than just the little neighborhood that I grew up in. Through that I began to start seeing the world." As Charles's sense of the world grew, he began to reconsider what should be important to him – he had to realize there was more than just the corner of his neighborhood.

So by reading and working, Charles would make it through his sentence; but as soon as he was released, Charles fell back into old ways: "the same vicious cycle of what I thought was a good time. My priorities were all screwed up." And so Charles became a part of what he terms the "revolving door" of prison life – until, that is, his most recent incarceration.

"This last incarceration I was sentenced to eight years for possession of controlled, dangerous substances, and I took a serious inventory of my life, of some of the loss around me, of the people that I grew up with, female companions, and how life in general was just changing… so when I came home from prison I elected to go into a transitional program, and through that process I got some insight and information on how to begin to lay the foundation of working on the things I needed to do for myself, and not anybody else." Charles entered Narc Anon, and made a choice. Charles puts the choice in clear terms: "It was live I will, or die I must. And I wanted to live."

Adding to Charles's motivation were two major events his life: the birth of his grandchildren, and the death of his own grandmother. The former, Charles says, really made him realize all that he had neglected in raising his daughter, the lessons and values which he had failed to teach her. The latter event was, in many ways, more profound for Charles, for it reminded Charles of what love meant, and how he had strayed from it: "...I had known my grandmother longer than I knew my biological mother, and me and my grandmother had a very strong relationship. No matter what I did, or where I went at, she was always there to support me, and if I was using drugs, hanging out in the streets, trying to do harm to other people, she still gave me that mental nourishment." Charles notes, quite plainly, that this often caused his grandmother to be an enabler, while he was in the midst of addiction. As she neared the end of her life, it was for the sake of her unconditional love that Charles wanted to change, wanted to become a better man.

Finally, on the night of his grandmother's death, Charles says that "when she passed away, she recognized that I wasn't the same individual that she had seen for the last twenty years of her life, and I was honored and privileged to have been present when she took her last breath." It was an insightful moment for Charles, when he realized that he had grown up. "Everybody has a stage in their life when they put all the BS behind them, and they begin to accept reality and life for what it is, and to do better things for themselves ...she [his grandmother] always said that I wasn't ignorant. That I just had to make choices on the things I had to do for myself."

Charles is now making those choices for himself. Though he has always regretted not getting his education when he was younger – he freely admits that it's harder the older you get – he does not lose himself in that regret; hence the title of his essay, *Appreciating My Past!* For now, Charles says it is enough to "just focus…on the goals that are in front of me. Not the long term goals, I'm just dealing with one step at a time. I want to ascribe to get my GED, … [and] to naturally take care of myself as I get older, and to be able to help my grandkids with their life, and instill some guiding principal into their life." Furthermore, Charles hopes that his story will reach more people than just his grandchildren; he hopes that his story will help anyone who has struggled as he has: "Someone took the time to guide me through my process [of recovery], and it was greater than having riches, or gold, and I just wanted to take this opportunity to give that which was freely given to me to someone that may have the same ill feeling about life, dysfunctional families, or just giving up hope." There is hope for everyone, Charles insists, and ways to change all of our lives, no matter what our past has been like. We can only learn by acknowledging where we have been.

Appreciating My Past! by Charles Vessells

It is very easy to be negative about my past mistakes and unhappiness, but it is much more healing to look at myself and my past in the light of experience, acceptance, and growth. My past is a series of lessons that advance me to a higher level of living and loving.

The relationships I've entered into, stayed in, or ended have taught me necessary lessons I needed to learn for myself. Through all that, I have emerged from the most painful of circumstances with very strong insights about who I am, and just what I want out of life. My mistakes? Necessary. My frustrations, failures, and sometimes stunbling attempts at growth and progress? All necessary too...but each step of the way, I've learned. I went through exactly the experiences I needed to, in order to become who I am today. Each step of the way, I've progressed.

Have you ever noticed a rose? It is majestic, but soft; precious, but strong; sturdy, but it possesses thorns. I, too, am like a rose, and possess unique, but common qualities. The thorns in my life are present by the grace of God. They are there as a witness of my past – but the light to my future. We need thorns to remind ourselves and others that we must go on daily in spite of everyday obstacles; life comes at you fast. Today, I have a positive attitude, and a God who is understanding, and helps me let go of the negative thoughts I may be harboring about my past circumstances. I am more precious in life that I realize. Today life is great, and each day I will enjoy it to the best of my ability with courage!

🔥Revolution
Making a Change

It is one thing to change yourself. Initiating self-change is certainly challenging – it is often one of the hardest things we could do in life. How much harder, then, is it to try and change others, when you lack even the little control that you have over your own choices? And to go bigger, to try and change the total reality in which you exist, may seem impossible.

There are some few in this world who have managed it; their passions, beliefs, and faith in a better tomorrow provoked change on national, even global levels. These men and woman of conviction have caused revolutions – total, radical changes to a society and culture. We study them in history books, and we wonder: what was the key to their success, success won where failure had dominated?

The answer – an answer both painfully simple and impossibly complicated – is that the greatest revolutionaries in this world had a simple, undying trust in the people whom they sought to serve. They weren't looking for power, they were looking for justice; they didn't seek change to better themselves, but to better others. Take, for a basic example, the American Revolution: the fight for independence and democracy was for nothing other than the right of a people to govern themselves, to *trust* the people to govern themselves. Gandhi's fight for India's independence rang of the same chords: the Indian people were to be trusted to lead themselves. The same can be said of the fall of the Apartheid in South Africa: it was a matter of asking the Afrikaans to trust the Africans in contributing to the successful governing of their mutual home. Even in religious institutions, we have seen Vatican II revolutionize the Catholic Church in that the clergy now trusted the laity to take part in liturgy, in theology, in the shaping of the Church.[2]

These are all, perhaps, obvious institutional examples. Ethical and cultural revolutions are somewhat harder to see – there is less visible and overt structure to change and can often take longer. Still, some come to mind, such the Civil Right's movement of the 1960's, where Black Americans called out for liberty, to be seen as Subjects, not Objects. Or, on a smaller scale, the Catholic Worker movement started by Dorothy Day in the early twentieth century, which showed the importance of solidarity. The Catholic Worker served the poor, but wasn't about welfare; rather, it was about people serving the needs of the oppressed, needs which they learned about from the oppressed themselves, not needs which were perceived from the outside.

Paulo Freire puts all of this in simpler terms, when he writes: "Political action on the side of the oppressed must be...action *with* the oppressed." In short, Freire believes liberation can only come from those who need to be liberated – it cannot be given. If liberation is "given" it is, in a sense, contradicting itself. Giving something implies that the receiver is an Object, passively receiving. Rather, liberty belongs to a Subject, who acts for oneself; thus, one must be a Subject who *takes* liberty. These numerous, successful revolutions all have one common thread, outside of trust: they all originated in the group which was oppressed, when they stood up, looked around, and began to question the cultural and societal institutions which they had always assumed were right and true.

Revolution, then, is an extension of conversion. The men and women in the previous section were part-way there; they saw that they were Objects, and are now seeking to be Subjects. Yet, what they have yet to do is challenge the bigger forces at work, the institutional oppression. The stories I give to you now take Conversion farther – by asking questions, making observations, and believing that change can happen on a larger scale than the individual.

I do not mean to imply that the other learners in this book are ignorant of these outside, beyond-their-control circumstances; rather, I doubt that, sincerely. I think the mere fact that so many voiced frustrations to me indicates an awareness of such. Saying otherwise is like saying that the humans Prometheus gave his torch to were ignorant of the heat, cold, and other forces of nature around them. However, until they had the knowledge of fire, there was little humanity could do to fight back.

Millenia later, there are still structures beyond our control, and the next five learners explicitly question those structures with their interviews and pieces. Janet Obeng, Dana Punnett, Angelo Adams, Gregory Whisonant, and Tyrone Peoples all believe that education will equip them with the tools necessary to alter society's institutions.

Janet, who comes from Ghana, sees our educational system from the outside; she asks how it is that we take such a gift for granted. She describes how our society functions, and the role which education plays in it; she even hints at a hidden caste system which education can break, *if* we use it properly.

Dana never liked being told what to do without good reason for it. Though that rebellious attitude resulted in her eventually dropping out, she's back now.

She understands the importance of education, but she's still challenging the world around her. She wrote of AIDS, and she chastises the wealthy that are ignoring the epidemic on the African continent.

Angelo has tried working within the system, but is frustrated by limitations. His desire to work in radiology required too much time away from his job – a job he would have needed to pay for those very classes, in addition to his home and other necessities. He sees literacy as liberating, especially on a cultural front. The poetry readings he attends have exposed him to an underground movement full of new ideas.

Gregory is the least subtle revolutionary of the group – *Revolution* is the title for his essay. He breaks down old assumptions about the Black Panther Party, and he asks his audience just what it is that they truly fear about change.

Finally, there is Tyrone. Tyrone was at Dr. Martin Luther King Jr.'s March on Washington, and Tyrone has seen Baltimore evolve over the years: desegregating schools, computer technology, and more. He is an artist, and his art captures that sense of cultural change, hope for the future, *revolution*.

Like conversion, revolution is a word with an intimidating connotation; it is linked to rebellion and violence. Yet none of the learners above advocate violence; all advocate awareness. Many of the learners I spoke to implied that their illiteracy prevented comprehension of the larger world around them. Newspapers were difficult to read, and few had cable with twenty-four-hour news channels. Information was sparse, and often unreliable. Yet, as the learners have improved their reading skills, they have gained new sorts of literacy: a literacy which is based in comprehension and hearing what hasn't been explicitly stated or written. Janet, Dana, Angelo, Gregory, and

Tyrone can now acutely feel the assumptions society makes about "people like Them" – or Others. Were more of the learner's friends and neighbors aware of those stereotypes, perhaps, they suggest, more would resist them.

We must see that the learners' desires for revolution come not from a place of violence, but from a place of love. Their personal encounters with revolution are all colored with love. Janet finds strength for her new life in American in the love of a friend. Dana will succeed for the love of her son, and Tyrone gave up his job, and paints, for the love of art. Indeed, the greatest revolutionaries of our time all worked from love: Dorothy Day, Ghandi, and Dr. King fought because they loved the men and women they were fighting for.

Let me return to the Freire quote from the introduction: he captures it the best when he writes: "And this fight [for change], because of the purpose given it by the oppressed, will actually constitute an act of love opposing the lovelessness which lies at the heart of the oppressors..." The greatest deeds to be done in this life can only result from love. Love – it's a revolutionary idea.

Janet Obeng

Janet Obeng is not only new to The Learning Bank, but also new to living in the United States. Until November of 2006 Janet lived with her family in Ghana, on the western coast of Africa. After less than half a year to adjust to the new culture and lifestyle, Janet then decided to take classes at The Learning Bank, beginning in May of this year. A shy, quiet woman, Janet is reputed to be one of the most dedicated students; it was her teacher, Ms. Baxter, who asked me to interview Janet, though Janet herself was hesitant to speak to me. Eventually, Janet agreed to the interview – only under the stipulation that she miss minimal class time, especially in Social Studies (which happens to be the class Ms. Baxter teachers, as well as Janet's favorite).

In many ways, Janet is still getting used to the educational process here in the United States. In Ghana, Janet completed what she calls "middle school," at home, in a private setting with a tutor. Of American schooling, Janet says: "The system here is much more… lenient. The privileges are here, but without paying. It is up to the…individual to make something of it." What Janet notes is that, because schooling was so expensive in Africa, those who pursued it had to do well simply to get their money's worth. In America, though education is more readily available, it's not (in Janet's personal experience) considered as important.

That rather lackadaisical attitude troubles Janet, somewhat. For her, it would be hard to place a value on a diploma; it's necessity to Janet is evident in her brief essay, Why is a High School Diploma Important? Moreover, the essay discusses her own personal desire to attend nursing college. Given so many opportunities now, in the U.S., Janet aims to make the most she can of them.

Yet, pursuing a dream of becoming a nurse has required a few changes on Janet's part. At one time, Janet explains to me, she really struggled with the math and science that would be needed in such a career: "When I could not find the answer to an [math] equation, I would quit. I did not like Math. I would not do it. But now, I learned to try again, to ask for help if I need it." This appreciation of those who have helped Janet comes through in her essay A True Friend, written about her best friend, Theresa, who still lives in Ghana. The persistence of friendship which Janet praises in the essay is echoed in the persistent way Janet approaches her studies; even when it's difficult, she will not give up.

Janet also places a very high value on the ability to read and write. In Ghana, Janet was taught English, and she speaks it quite well today; though in our interview she seems to take extra-care in choosing her words, speaking slowly and intentionally. However, it is reading and writing that Janet desires to master, saying that it helps her to study better, as she processes the information she learns. Janet also hopes to start reading more in her free time. In Ghana, Janet states that she "...liked reading. It wasn't much novels, but anything I else I got." Now, with a greater access to novels and books here, she wants to read more, and learn more by doing so.

Ultimately, Janet continues her education to be an example to her children. By becoming a nurse, she feels she could show her children all the possibilities out there for them, as they go on with their schooling. "It's important to be educated," Janet proclaims, "because it makes one think....fast. The more you are in the classroom, are being taught, the more you can process and understand everything...[This] helps in the office, or even in the house, or really every area of life."

A few weeks after this interview, I was granted the opportunity to hear Janet speak at the closing ceremony for The Learning Bank. After a handful of learners had taken the opportunity to speak, Janet (who was advancing in math), tentatively raised her hand. Janet received a nod of approval from Ms. Butler, and made her way to the front of the room.

Janet was positively beaming – her bright, white smile stretched across her face as she spoke, her cheeks darkened just enough to show a blush. And, in her patient and determined way of speaking, Janet thanked all her teachers, and all who worked at The Learning Bank. I could see, in that moment, her joy in being able to not only educate herself, but succeed and advance in that education – quickly, efficiently. At the end of her speech, Janet said "I hope, every much, to see everyone next cycle." As the learners clapped for her, I knew without a doubt that Janet would provide for them a model, an image of success – proof, if you will, of just how far education can carry you.

A True Friend by Janet Obeng

A true friend is one who stays with his or her partner till death. There are some friends who associate themselves with their partners, because of what they will gain, but a true friends gives all that he has, even to the last penny.

Opportunists will remain friends for as long as you have money and fame, but a true friend stays with the partner in times of trouble, and at times when they commit mistakes and challenge their friends to pursue further in times of discouragement.

I have a friend called Theresa. She has been my friend for five years, and has done a lot for me and my family. Theresa is always there to support me when I have a problem. She also advises and consoles me in times of disappointments. Theresa is not a friend who disappears when there is trouble, but is always present to give advice, and directs me to take appropriate action when there is trouble. Theresa is kind and selfless. She shares whatever she has with me without any hope for a return favor.

Why is a High School Diploma Important?
by Janet Obeng

The high school diploma is important because obtaining it will lead one to a higher level in education. This diploma grants a student the right to enter college, and from that level he or she can pursue a professional degree.

The system of our economy demands well educated personal in order to work in offices, govern our states, educate the illiterate, and doctor in hospitals. One cannot achieve these professions without a high school diploma. Also, obtaining it creates a chance of one's salary to be increased.

Personally, I see the need to obtain this diploma since I want to be a nurse; and if possible, pursue a higher level than that. This can be possible, if I obtain a high school diploma.

Dana Punnett

Dana Punnett is a tall, no-nonsense, take-no-prisoners-type of woman. This rather fits, since she currently works as a security guard. One of the first learners to sit and speak with me, Dana freely and bluntly admitted that, when she was younger, she undervalued her education. Of the attitude she took while attending school, Dana said: "…I used to always think it was just some place to go, that we had to go. But I never knew the reason, nobody ever told me the reason *why* I had to go to school…I thought it was like a daycare or something." Dana is not unreasonable; were she told, as a teenager, all the real benefits to earning a diploma and attending college, she surely would have made the effort to complete high school. Yet no one ever did so; as a result of this "just because" attitude towards education, Dana never really put her whole effort into learning.

It's not an uncommon story, really. As Dana implies in her first essay, *My Path to Success*, it was easy for her to lose focus in high school without a real motive to commit to learning. She lacked the encouragement necessary to pursue it, and, in the end, thought she could make her way in life just as well without it.

Now, Dana is older, and between her job and her young child, she has a number of responsibilities which need her to focus on the now, and yet still plan for the future. Today, Dana sees her education in a much more pragmatic light than she did as a teen – which was really not all that long ago. Dana explained her matter-of-fact reason for returning to her studies: "I want to go to college…my job could lose their contract in the year 2009…" After a moment's pause, thinking, Dana adds: "I'm kind of sick of doing security, too." At the very least, Dana realizes that a better education could mean financial security, something she realizes is worth the investment of time it takes to study and learn. Yet, it is more; working hard could allow Dana to find a passion, a job she can care for, and not just something which pays the bills.

So now, at The Learning Banks, Dana is working very hard to stay focused, to learn, and especially to learn how to write. She attends the Evening Program at The Learning Bank, spending each of her Tuesdays and Thursdays in class, even after a long day of work. Whether in math or in science, Dana commits her whole attention to the teacher. Outspoken and determined, Dana is unafraid to raise her hand and ask for explanations, going over and over a geometry problem until it all makes sense, and when it does, her self-satisfaction is almost palpable.

Geometry aside, Dana tells me she works the hardest in her reading classes. Dana's greatest obstacle in writing is "trying not to write the way I talk. That is extremely hard...in an essay. In my personal writing, yeah, I write the way I talk." It would seem that Dana creates a divide between her personal writing, and her professional writing. Yet there are some things which overlap, namely, a very down-to-earth sensibility which influences her writing, her reading, and her professional goals.

In the long run, Dana has big plans: she wants to go to college for psychology, but not, she is clear and quick to state, to be a psychologist. Rather, in *My Path to Success*, Dana describes her desires to open her own salon or childcare center, yet Dana also says she would want to "work with troubled teens, somebody that I can use my past to...help them. Sometimes we have older people that try to help younger people, but that don't always work..." Using her own life experience, Dana understands the importance of reaching out to the youth, and reaching out in a way that the youth can relate to. She doesn't want to be like one of the adults who expected her to follow rules "just because." Rather, she wants to give empirical proof of the importance of being educated. "I would take them through my past," Dana says, "and show them my paycheck...if they could come see my house and see my bills and know that I'm really struggling...education is the only way if you want better financial stability." Nothing will speak more strongly to a teen, Dana believes, than the sight of a paycheck next to the bill for rent and utilities.

Such desires are echoed in the second essay, written for Dana's Social Studies class, *If I had a Million Dollars*. There, Dana shows an awareness of the needs of others across the globe with a discussion of the A.I.D.S. crisis in Africa; furthermore, she clearly describes the need for education, providing links between education and income, driving home her point. The essay really challenges the reader to assess their priorities; Dana even goes so afar as to point the blame at parents who fail to really encourage their children in school.

Dana, at least, will not make that mistake with her child when he's old enough for school. In the meanwhile, she will work to achieve job security – not just a job in security.

My Path To Success by Dana Punnett

My path to success will take a lot of focus and power. Due to my rough past, I now have a late start on my journey to success. I looked at my environment, and noticed that it's hard being a minority. Since then, I have opened my eyes to discover that I will not be a product of my environment. I will set my standards high to ensure that my son will never be subjected to my past.

Planning this path has been easy; the execution, on the other hand, has been trying. This spring I have enrolled in The Learning Bank to get my G.E.D. It has been coming along very well. The work is not difficult and the teachers are understanding, but my struggle is to overcome losing focus. I have been walking this path that I have started, and I will not stop until I finish.

Upon proudly receiving my diploma, I will move on to furthering my education in college, and then entering the fields of childcare, cosmetology, or barbering. My ultimate goal is to turn my house into a Childcare Center. I am also going to open my long awaited dream: a salon that's out of this world. It will cater to the needs of people of all kinds. This is my path to success, and staying focused will help me see my vision clearer.

If I had One Million Dollars by Dana Punnett

If I was given one million dollars to spend, I think the only thing to do with the money would be to donate it, because I could not spend it on myself, family members, or a friend. I would donate to two different organizations. I would give half a million to one organization, and give the other half to another.

The first five hundred thousand would go to the research for developing a cure for the H.I.V. and A.I.D.S. virus. There are a lot of wealthy people that are not giving money to support the studies of this important research process. It would be an honor for me to give as much money as possible to keep us on this earth as long as we can. Without a cure, this deadly epidemic will wipe out the human race.

The other half of million I would spend on a random minority individual's future, because education is the best gift in the world. Sometimes parents cannot afford school expenses, which is due to low incomes in their households. A lot of people fail to realize in most cases the reason there are low-income families is also from a lack of education. Then there are parents who just do not stress the importance of education. If I had the money to change one person's future, I wouldn't think twice about giving that money.

In conclusion, with me receiving one million dollars, I think I would have spent it well. Killing two birds with one stone, I would have changed the future of the earth, and invested in my mental wealth. Now what better way to spend my money than to help someone?

Angelo Lewis

The philosophy Angelo Lewis has towards education can be summed up in one word: Freedom. This is clearly stated in the main theme of his poem, *Free*, which describes illiteracy as a roadblock which he must overcome to realize his destiny. This roadblock, for him, impinges on his career, on his financial success, and on his total sense of self. When I ask why he decided to attend The Learning Bank and get his GED, forty-five year old Angelo answers, very simply: "I had a problem with being illiterate, and I wanted to do something about that." Where others would list outside pressures as motivations (such as jobs, children, or parole), Angelo is here of his own accord. Angelo wants his GED for his own well-being, his own sense of accomplishment and his own personal *Free*dom.

Angelo is very goal-oriented, easily acknowledging problems and working to find the best solution for them. During his time spent in the evening program at the Learning Bank, Angelo has taken classes in each of the areas that individuals are tested on during the GED. The two classes Angelo is currently enrolled in, Algebra and Language Arts, are the classes which will help him pass the final two sections. Ever moving towards his goals and desires, Angelo plans to take the GED test again at the end of June.

However, passing the GED is just the next step for Angelo. He has been at The Learning Bank since July of 2005. He has enjoyed his time in class: "the overall learning experience has been good...I like to participate, and I am making it a priority to finish." After completing the program and earning his GED, Angelo hopes to switch career paths, going from being a truck driver to possibly selling insurance; originally, Angelo had investigated the prospect of being a radiology technician. However, being practical as always, and researching the career, Angelo discovered that he would need to quit his full-time job in order to take up the classes that were required: "I don't think that would be feasible for me to quit my job to obtain… [a degree]." He speaks without resentment, or regret – that it just how it is. Angelo is too pragmatic to resent the facts of the present; when he encounters the end of one career path, he won't waste time lamenting the loss, but find move on to the next one.

If Angelo regrets anything, it is his former experience in school. "I didn't understand the seriousness of my education," Angelo says, "I guess due to the environment in which I was raised." As a result, Angelo feels as though he neglected the many other potential jobs that were available for him as a younger man. "My attitude about acquiring a decent job…that's changed. That's something that you have to have, you know, in order to take other steps in other directions. To have your high school diploma – GED -- is a must in order to, you know, go to another school, or… pick up another career…your education can open doors for you to experience different things." So it isn't just career opportunities which Angelo seeks, but also new experiences –*enriching* experiences unlike anything else he's had before. Still, as Angelo advances towards his future, he knows one thing for certain: "You have to put yourself in a position to make yourself valuable to an employer. So you have to *know* something."

Now, Angelo is immersing himself in literacy; from attending poetry readings to making sure he reads the finance section of the newspaper every morning. He recognizes the importance of writing, and how it can help: "I have a lot of thoughts sometimes and I, I should just start writing them down."

In fact, doing just that resulted in his poem, *Free*: "This is basically the first poem I wrote. It seemed to come very, very easy to me...I'd just think of things and just put it on paper." Angelo's greatest struggle, he tells me, is with spelling – but then, Angelo always keeps a dictionary on hand. It's just another practical way to keep learning.

Free by Angelo Lewis

Who am I
What is me
Is it because I don't know
my History

Is it because I don't know
my destiny
and I cannot read or write
my History

Is my life without a destiny

Well

My illiteracy constantly
Remind me that my
Education is the only
thing to set me

Free

Gregory Whisonant

"What's wrong with a change?" Gregory Whisonant asks in the opening paragraph of his essay, *Revolution.* Yet Gregory dares the reader to accept much more than mere change. Rather, Gregory challenges his readers to look past common knowledge, or what they *think* they know, to change their preconceptions – to revolutionize their assumptions.

Gregory is twenty-eight years old, and a soft-spoken man of few words; his interest in politics goes back quite some time. He reads a great deal of literature about philosophy and politics; this alone defies the average stereotype of someone who has not graduated from high school. Much of the information in *Revolution* came from authors such as Assata Shakur, Huey P. Newton, Bobby Seale, and Fred Hampton. Most of the information about the Black Panthers in Gregory's essay comes from the first three; Gregory has always been impressed by the strength of the authors' convictions. "I just was curious," Gregory says of his initial attraction to politics and power, "I was basically curious about all the type of things they be talking about."

Gregory has also read about religion, most extensively about the Nation of Islam, which he believes holds similar themes of power and justice in common with the Black Panthers. "I try to learn about all different types [of religions]," Gregory sats, "and understand them...I don't really have a certain religion [of my own]." Ideas intrigue Gregory more than anything else, and these continue to stimulate his desire to read and learn.

Yet, this is the sort of learning Gregory feels he can only do on his own; he tells me he didn't enjoy many aspects of his high school education: "I liked... [school], but I wasn't going to like taking orders – I didn't like other people telling me what to do, other than my parents." Shades of Gregory's interest in revolutionary ideology can be seen in this attitude, especially when he explains how his parents tried to keep him in school: "My father always told me to get my education while it is free, but he never sat down and explained to me the reasons why I should go to school, stay in school." He sought the reasons for the rules and power exerted over him, just as the authors he reads seek reasons for the way power and law work on a national level. Gregory is not about to obey an institution simply because it says to.

Now, however, Gregory sees value in formal education, and in earning a diploma. As he explains: "I'm trying to get my life into order…trying to obtain my GED. I think I'm getting old enough that I should've had it already." Despite his own rebellion against schooling, Gregory would caution others against doing the same. The greatest pitfall for high school students today, Gregory says, is "trying to run with the crowd. Trying to do everything your friends are doing and not staying focused on school." In a way, simply running with the crowd is the same as mindlessly obeying the rules of school – "the crowd" is simply another, more informal institution trying to boss you around. Gregory observes than an education can at least help you to think for yourself, and develop your own ideas.

That is not to say that Gregory doesn't still sympathize with the frustrations of school for a young student; he just wants others to realize that, in the long run, school will help far more than it hinders: "Even though it seems like most of the subjects that you deal with in school, you're not gonna need ever in life, it's definitely worth staying in school." The authors whom Gregory admires were all in high school once, and were able to turn an otherwise ordinary education into something much, much more. It is education that creates awareness. That awareness, in turn, lets us recognize and seize the power which will beget revolutions.

Revolution by Gregory Whisonant

Let's talk about the word Revolution. What does it mean? Well, when you ask some people about this word, or to define this word, they will say or think of violence, racists, war, or "crazy black people." But when you look this word up, all it means is change. So what's wrong with change? There is nothing wrong with change; but the government wants you to think so.

This word revolution, or the word revolutionary, was adopted by the Black Panther Party around 1966, which was originally called the Black Panther Party for Self Defense. The black panther was used as a symbol because it was a powerful image, and the "self defense" was employed to distinguish the party's philosophy from the dominant nonviolent theme of the civil rights movement.

Not every thing that you hear about this organization is true. It was said to be a violent group of black people; not true, the members of the party were only violent when they had to be. They did not believe in turning the other cheek. The Black Panther Party came about to be the voice of all the oppressed people – not only blacks, though the blacks were their aim.

This organization did a lot for communities. The first such program was the *Free Breakfast for the Children Program*, which spread outward from being operated at one small Catholic church, in San Francisco. But the government doesn't tell you that. Yes, the Black Panther Party started *Free Breakfast for the Children*. But then the FBI got mad, and tried to start the same type of program for public schools. The FBI said that the Black Panther program was nothing more than a propaganda tool to carry out its communist agenda, and denounced the party as communist outlaws bent on overthrowing the U.S. government.

Now, you tell me who's the crazy ones?

See nowadays, the black people are so naïve that they can't see how much of an impact we are on this world. We are the highest consumers in the world, but we can't even run our own companies. We are too busy with jewelry, cars, and other things that don't matter. Governments all over the world are making it hard for people to live and no one says anything about it. Baltimore Gas and Electric is going up fifteen percent. Why? The gas price is almost three dollars a gallon - why? What about people that make minimum wage with kids - how will they live? So does the government care? I think not!!

So this is the time when we need to stand up for all the people in this situation, not just blacks, but all minority groups. One of the problems is that the community does not have a structured organization or vehicle which serves its needs and represents the people's interests. You can no more have effective politics without a structured organization than you can have a man without his shadow.

To me, a lot of this starts with religion. This was something that we are giving up to, so we can not fault anyone else but God. Heaven and Hell is only what we make it. If you do well in life, it will feel like Heaven because it's as if you have no worries, and if so, they are not that bad. But if you grew up like me, it would feel like Hell. Don't get me wrong, there were some Heaven-times, but there were more Hell-times. Don't let it get you down, because when you're doing your best with life that's all that counts. Never give up on your dreams, or your hopes, or your people. The struggle is ordained, it will always be here, and it could be worse.

Keep on pushing!!!
POWER to All the Struggling People!!!!

Tyrone Peoples

In the middle of the summer, I was privileged
to view a showing of Tyrone Peoples's work, hosted
by The Learning Bank. Spread across the walls was
a myriad of paintings. The artwork ranged from
grayscale profiles of famous black musicians and artists,
to nature scenes with snowcapped mountains and thick
evergreen trees, to colorful bursts of flowers in full
bloom.

Talking to Tyrone Peoples is rather like seeing
history come alive, again - in a way, Tyrone seems to
come from a different era. A tall, elegant man, Tyrone
is one of the most visible learners, and comes into
The Learning Bank each day in crisply-ironed button-
down shirts and neatly creased slacks which hit just
above pointed, black shoes. He speaks in long, complex,
articulate sentences; each phrase is packed with
information from a life that has seen the turmoil of the
sixties become the struggles of the present, and viewed
it all with the memory and clarity of an artist's eye.

Art has been Tyrone's passion since he was three
years old; it is his great, consuming passion. At one
point, as I spoke with him, he chided me gently for
not having asked which mediums he works in. When
I did ask, he listed over half a dozen, including oil
paints, acrylics, water colors, pen and ink, ink wash,
chalk, wood, and clay: "and any other medium I see,"
Tyrone added, "[that] I might want to do, I'll do it." He
currently runs his own small artwork business, which
sells his works, along with tee shirts of his own design,
as well. The business is small, and was slow to establish
itself, but Tyrone doesn't mind. His art has always been
his dream, and though he may miss the income of a
regular nine-to-five job, Tyrone will declare to anyone:
"I don't want to miss my dream."

The stories behind the art – behind Tyrone's life – serve to enhance artwork itself. Tyrone points to one painting: two young children wash dishes with their back to us, while bubbles and suds overflow the sink. He calls attention to the background. The scene of childhood playfulness is set in a drop of water on brown, cracked payment. The scene is memory, Tyrone explains to us, set in the brother's teardrop as he cries by his sister's murdered body: thus the title, "Teardrops and Memories." Tyrone then explains that a nearby, smaller print depicting the shadow of a man and the bars of a jail is the murderer – titled "My Prayer." The shadow's hands are raised in anguish, clutching at the bars; he is begging, it seems, for something like forgiveness. Finally, he told us about a third piece (absent from the showing) called "Genocide." It depicts a gun, Tyrone says, – the gun that shot the sister. Genocide would complete the set, telling a story of guilt, grief, and sorrow.

Another print depicts the faces of Dr. Martin Luther King, Jr., Nelson Mandela and Malcolm X juxtaposed over one another. In a dark corner of the painting, a line of Black men march by, each one holding a sign which says "I am a man." The parallels between the American civil rights movement, and the struggle of South Africa are obvious, the leaders all charismatic, and the total picture engrossing and heartrending. As I stare at these pieces, I see the life stories of Tyrone jump off of them, his experiences in life are the oil in the paint, the color of the hues.

Tyrone had to travel a long road before he was able to pursue his passion. As one of fifteen children in his immediate family, Tyrone talked of the struggles his family had in the sixties; amid political turmoil there were also personal and financial issues. When asked what he remembered most clearly about his early school

years, he replied: "That takes you back. In the sixties…
not having the proper clothes to wear, and still having
to go to school; some of the teachers that were there
wasn't being fair. And then when you were put in…say,
a vocational class, [and] they really didn't know where
to put you, so you was just moved around, you know,
they did various things like pass you by your age…"

Tyrone made it very clear that he had few good
memories of his primary schooling: "You ask me what
did I enjoy in school? Well, actually…elementary I
didn't enjoy, because of some of the stuff that was
going on back in the sixties. You had people being
bussed to different schools, you lived right up the street
from a school, then you're being taken by a bus from
here to across town, you know what I mean, so I didn't
enjoy that, that was a lot of transition in that time." Yet,
at the end of all that, Tyrone adds with the hint of a
smile: "But my favorite subject from that time in school
was Art."

Things grew more complicated for Tyrone as he
entered junior high and high school. Though Tyrone
did go all the way through twelfth grade in a vocational
high school, he did not graduate. He points to a
number of contributing factors: "Then you get up into
the seventies, junior high, well aged fifteen I had my
first child, which was a struggle. So I was in and out,
in and out of school…I had to work, so that took me
out of class, and by the time I made up my mind to
come back, I was really screwed, already, for my grades,
and I never could make it back up. And that's…why I
couldn't get a diploma." Tyrone does not, however, look
upon any of this with bitterness, or shame. To him, the
story is one frequently heard for men of his generation.
Despite not receiving a diploma, Tyrone was able to
find a steady job with a pharmaceutical plant, where he
worked for seventeen years.

"I worked my way from a packer, to a machine operator…You worked with a lot of numbers and all, you had a chart to keep, which was pretty cool, man…." As Tyrone describes his job, much of the number crunching was done by rote – plus, Tyrone had always been strong in math when he was in school. He quickly became accustomed to the routine of his position, yet he says, "I never stopped drawing during that job… I had a plan to work there about seventeen, maybe even twenty years, save up some money, and resign and pursue my dream. So after seventeen years, that's what I did. I resigned, pulled my money out of my 401K… and got a little tee shirt business."

Though Tyrone is now working as an artist, with a fair amount of success, he still felt the pull to complete his education – but on his own terms. So two years ago, Tyrone entered The Learning Bank, and has since started using his art to facilitate his studies, and vice-versa. For example, The Learning Bank once had a presentation about the Buffalo Soldiers; Tyrone has since done pieces of art about them. Or, once Tyrone was investigating some major figures of the civil rights movement, including President Kennedy, Coretta Scott King, and Martin Luther King, Jr., with the plan of creating clay busts of them. When Tyrone was then given an assignment to write about a major political figure, he chose Dr. King, who was proving to be the most appealing figure in Tyrone's research.

Indeed, Dr. King has always stood out prominently in Tyrone's mind. Tyrone remembers being a young boy of seven, and attending Dr. King's March on Washington, where he gave his famous *I Have a Dream* speech: "It was a lot of people there, a lot of people… think that it was just all black people, one race. It was all kind of races there. And I never forgot that … because it was a sea of people, and you could hear his voice miles away. It was one of the most exciting points of my life, to be involved in something like that. Of course, when I was seven I had no idea that stuff like that would go down in history, you know." To this day, the history that Tyrone experienced as a boy influences his artwork – and his return to his education has helped to deepen his appreciation of history. "I check out everything…" Tyrone explains, commenting on how he uses reading and writing in his art, "I look up certain things, certain artists, some of the history that I was talking about, I look at all sorts of history. I know things now that I didn't even know I knew, since I've been here [at The Learning Bank]."

Furthermore, Tyrone is utterly unafraid to talk about what he terms a "handicap" – his lack of a diploma: "But just talking to you, just meeting me, without doing this [project], you probably never would have known my handicap. A lot of people don't know….and a lot of people with this type of handicap, they don't want people to know about it. Sometimes it's embarrassment, sometimes it's fear. And those are things that keep you, and the average person, from learning and picking up more and going back to school…that's why I'm here."

Always thinking about the future, Tyrone discusses his plans for when he does graduate with a GED: "Once I get out of here, my plan, if everything goes right, I want to do a little teaching. Teach the youth, or anybody who wants to learn about Art." Just as Dr. King taught people about his dream, so Tyrone wants to teach others about his personal dream.

He has even taken the first step by hosting the art show at The Learning Bank. In one corner, on a clean, white canvas, I see Tyrone teaching learners how to paint beautiful, simple, colorful flowers. One woman laughs as she tries it – "I've never been an artist, before" she says. Tyrone smiles; perhaps seeing an artist in all of us. It's clear that Tyrone has a lot to show the world, and he intends for the world to see it all. When I thanked Tyrone for sharing his story, he simply laughed and said: "Well you ain't got half of it…"

by Tyrone Peoples

🔥Solidarity
A Mutual Fight

I will be honest; knowing that I am a member of the privileged class in this country, it was intimidating for me to write of injustices. After all, I am not someone who deals with injustices first hand; I listen, I learn, but I do not suffer except in sympathy. Empathy is beyond my realm of experience. To the oppressed, I am the Other. If the revolution must be theirs, what place do I, and others with privilege, have in it?

Again, Freire answers this: solidarity. Freire calls oppressors to ignore the differences of Self and Them, and join in with the oppressed:

> "[Solidarity] is a radical posture...The oppressor is solidary with the oppressed only when he stops regarding the oppressed as an abstract category and sees them as persons... when he stops making...gestures and risks an act of love. True solidarity is found only in the plentitude of this act of love..."

We see a mythological example of this risk in Prometheus. His rebellion against Zeus earned him great punishment. Of course, Prometheus knew his risk would have dire consequences, and yet he continued on because of love. Prometheus saw humanity's potential, and allowed himself to be humbled so they could have the tool they needed to become great: fire.

It is not easy to be in solidarity. I am reminded of a sign I came across in New Orleans, on a trip there to do service work, which read: "Solidarity, not charity." Yet, I would venture to contradict the slogan, memorable though it is. True charity -- not writing a check, or giving away handouts – is nothing less than love for all those around us. *Charity*, we seem to have forgotten, comes from *caritas*, a Latin word used in Christianity to describe the unending love which the Christ is meant to have for humankind. This love is not limited to God, or Christianity. It is a love founded in the dignity of humankind, and the love which an oppressor will cultivate for the oppressed in response to the act of love which is the oppressed's revolution. To see each other as equals, to love each other as equals: that is the mark of a just society.

The three stories here are each offered by someone who has, to some degree, privilege; yet he or she uses that privilege to help those without it. Leroy Young, Yvonne Butler, and myself have the privilege of an education which the learners at The Learning Bank do no have. Leroy and Yvonne both describe their choice to make adult education and literacy a career – indeed, from their narratives, it feels like a vocation and calling. For myself, I have tried my best to show in a personal literacy narrative the transformation I underwent, where education, and in turn literacy, started as personal burdens and instead became issues of equity and justice.

It took me a long time to see my own personal privilege; and it took me longer, still, to understand what I could do to work for justice, for equality, for love.

Leroy, Yvonne, and I are three people with different positions in The Learning Bank, different backgrounds, different points of view – even our writing styles are different. Nevertheless, we are united with a common passion: the learners. We see every single learner uniquely, individually. I add our writings here to prove that anyone, from any background, can join in the revolution. You don't have to be a titan to bear Prometheus's torch.

LeRoy J. Young, Jr., *Assistant Director of the Learning Bank of C.O.I.L., Inc. (November, 2006 – present)*

My road to the Learning Bank and adult literacy actually began thirty-four years ago, when I was introduced to a fascinating word: "andragogy." As a fledging member of the former Homestead-Montebello Center (HMC) of Antioch College, I was required to read various materials that would prepare me to become a facilitator, or "artist," in the school of adult learning. I subsequently became quite enamored with the process that focused on adults as being pro-active partners and critical thinkers in the learning interchange. Or as Brookfield (1986) so aptly describes: "facilitating learning is a transactional encounter in which learner desires and educator priorities will inevitably interact and influence each other." From that point on, I was hooked on Malcolm Knowles' theory, techniques, and assumptions underlying the practice of adult learning.

As a result of my HMC-Antioch adjunct faculty activities, I subsequently experienced adult learning in venues ranging from anti-poverty programs to community colleges, and finally with the Baltimore City government. It was during an on-loan assignment to Mayor Kurt L. Schmoke's literacy initiative, Baltimore Reads, that I was introduced to the wonderfully positive work of The Learning Bank. So in reality, my road to The Learning Bank began eighteen years ago in 1989. It was a road filled with adult learners who were highly motivated to achieve a level of academic self-sufficiency that would make a significant difference in their and their families' lives, as well as, contributing to the community's future vitality. It was a road distinguished by educators, volunteers, and patrons who realized the importance of providing a reflective learning domain that fostered self-directed learning skills and established a humane, physically and psychologically conducive learning climate.

The original "journey," or loan, to Baltimore Reads was supposed to last for one year. However, one year stretched to nine – nine rewarding years interacting with adult learners and refining my practice. The Baltimore City helm of leadership changed, and I returned to my role as a Department of Housing, Training Officer. I continued in that role as a "corporate educator" for a few more years and retired from City government after thirty years of service. Semi-retirement began, and my Learning Bank journey began again. My life-long learning experience continued as the andragogy road crew constructed a new on-ramp -- I assumed the role of Assistant Director. A few things have changed. Some of the adult learners are younger, some staff has moved on, and a state of the art learning facility exists. But one thing remains the same; The Learning Bank of COIL, Inc. still remains as a shining beacon for Baltimore City's and Maryland's adult learning population.

Yvonne Butler, *Evening Program Coordinator at The Learning Bank of C.O.I.L., Inc., (1997-Present)*

My relationship with Literacy began at The Learning Bank of C.O.I.L, 10 years ago. Judy Hickey, who was the Instructional Specialist at that time, convinced me that I could help students reach their academic goals. Since I did not have any experience teaching in the classroom, I was reluctant to try. Hickey assured me that I was a teacher, even though I was not in an "official classroom." During that time, I was working with The Women's Housing Coalition as a counselor of three transitional houses and the resident manager of the first Single Room Occupancy (SRO) in the state of Maryland.

Working with women who were in transition from homelessness, drugs, abuse, mental health, and behavior problems was rewarding, but there were times that I felt that it was difficult to gauge successes because of the many layers of despair and the feelings of unworthiness that was a constant enemy of change and completion for many of them.

So, after a lot of thought, I decided to try to be in service to the learners at The Learning Bank. My biggest surprise was that I would be working with The Sisters of Mercy, humble, gracious, diligent, devoted, and committed nuns.

This prospect frightened me because I had never been in the company of such "holiness." As a matter of fact, Sister Judith first greeted me by saying that, "they couldn't do this by themselves." For whatever calming reason, I knew that it would be okay.

Actually, it was more than okay. Everybody worked for the learners to succeed. We had teachers, volunteers and tutors who feared the area because of the vicious drug trafficking across the street and in front of the door, but still braved the trek it took to get into the building.

Once that threshold of fear and destruction was crossed, we entered a building that is commonly called "on oasis" in this block, and the work began. Unlike the despair and the feelings of unworthiness, our students came here so that they could improve their literacy skills, and improve the quality of there life. Most of them were frightened, but they still wanted more instruction. It was not hard to make that transition from my previous work, because I discovered that they came into the classroom with a lot of the same problems. The difference was that I could see them progress. In my previous work, there was only the hope that my clients would use the tools and strategies given them to evolve.

At The Learning Bank, I would immediately know because students would improve their writing, reading and math skills. Many of them received their GEDs, and many just wanted be able to write a money order. These successes may by small to some people, and a lot of the community may feel that this population of people will never achieve, or want better. But who knows anyone who doesn't want better, or to achieve something? The best part of this journey was learning to help the students *and* to trust that they had everything they needed internally to forge ahead with work and diligence.

Lorraine Cuddeback, *Intern and Volunteer Tutor at The Learning Bank of C.O.I.L., Inc. (May 2006-present)*

Previous to my first Report Card Day, I had only received grades in bright red pen on my tests and quizzes; but I vaguely perceived from the level of tension over this set of grades that much more was at stake. One by one, each student was sent out to a lone desk in the hall. The Principal sat there; she was a nice woman (or so I assumed, since all nuns were supposed to be nice) whose dominant feature was white – white hair, white skin, white shirt, white hands. I watched as she removed the report card from the envelope, and her alabaster finger ran along a column with letters printed on it, each one next to a subject. I saw "Math," "Science," and "Language Arts," each one with a judgmental letter next to it. It was the last subject that caught my eye – in a line of A's and B's, there was a single C+ next to Language Arts. It jumped out at me, a harsh letter not at all redeemed by the plus sign next to it.

Next to me, The Principal spoke. The words "strong," "grades" and "student" grazed my ears, but the ones that truly stuck were: "could maybe work harder in Language Arts." I blushed with a furious shame, and my eyes began to prick with tears. I do work hard. I do I do I do I do.

I vowed right then — before even knowing the word vow — that I would never let myself get another C+ again.

The passage above was written in the fall of my sophomore year of college. As a part of the Writing Center Theory and Practice class, I was asked to compose a memoir – specifically, a *literacy* memoir. As I dug through my memories, looking for those Big Moments of my past concerning reading and writing, I found myself preoccupied with school while my classmates wrote about their favorite books, or stories their grandparents told them. Yet I was drawn to the classroom, to the epic struggles of my childhood and adolescence.

To be perfectly honest, I couldn't tell you many specifics of what I was taught in my first year at St. Matthias School – my grammar school for grades one through eight. I might mention Mad Minutes: a series of thirty addition and subtraction problems which had to be completed within a minute. I could also tell you that my teacher had a chart hanging on the wall, where she put stars next to the name of each student who successfully completed a Mad Minute, and that I never received a single one. I might describe the Book-It Club to you, which asked us to read five books a month; in exchange, we would get vouchers for a free, personal pizza at Pizza Hut. And if I think, very hard, I might vaguely recall a science experiment which consisted of planting a lima bean in a Styrofoam cup of dirt, in the hopes that it would grow a plant. I could also tell you that my teacher, because I wasn't paying strict attention to her directions, took the cup from my hands and threw it all out, leaving me out of the experiment and without a plant on the windowsill.

So yes, I was taught addition and subtraction. I was taught how to read, and how to spell. I was taught about the sun, soil, and plants. But what I *learned*, the message that I internalized, (which is so evident in the passage above) was that school was a competition. I learned stars were only given to those who deserved them by passing the Mad Minute tests, I learned that rewards came from reading as much as possible, as quickly as possible, and I learned to always follow exactly what the teacher told me, or I would be embarrassed in front of the rest of the class.

Five years later, in the sixth grade, school had hardly changed for me:

"*Excuse me?*"

"*You received a C on the paper, Lorraine, because you wrote in the second person, and the passive voice. That's not acceptable.*" The words were patronizing, drenched and dripping in "*You should've been smart enough to know this.*"

"*It's not? I...I'm sorry, I'm confused. I'm not sure I know what the second person or the passive voice is.*"

"*Oh, well....*" Surprise registered in the blue eyes behind wire rimmed glasses, and the smooth voice lost its snobbery while she grasped for words. "*Well, the second person is any use of personal pronouns, Lorraine. You, I, We...and the passive voice is, well, it's hard to describe.*"

"*I didn't know I wasn't allowed to use them.*"

"*You didn't? They're standard rules, every student should know that.*" A giant bouffant of white-blonde hair shook itself free of the pesky student, and with no more than that I was dismissed.

These words of wisdom came from Mrs. Saltzbart, who soundly won the title of Worst Teacher, Ever. The C on my final paper pulled my grade down to a C+ for the marking period. Tears of fury pushed through my eyelids when I saw that letter, the letter I'd vowed against as a first grader. And for what? A rule my teacher could hardly define.

I turned away from Mrs. Saltzbart and returned to my desk; though it had been years since I cried in school, I could feel the tears slip through my lids, and I clenched my teeth with the effort of resistance. I would not cry; I would not show weakness. There was a spotlight on me, as the entire class witnessed my losing battle with The Rules. They could see failure branded in the C upon my brow, and I was sure they were secretly mocking me for it.

I sat at my desk: jaw locked, eyes red, and chin high. These rules did not rule me – that much I was sure of – but they ruled my grades. Those grades which mattered so much; those precious A's which I continually struggled to earn.

*Though I valued my independence as a writer, I valued high
marks more. One would have to bow to the other, and the
choice had already been made for me.*

*As I opened my English book to the page that the rest of
my classmates were staring at, I decided that the breaking
of an old vow called for the creation of a new one. I would
learn these "rules," I would become fluent in their language.
I would practice them, use them, manipulate them. I would
conquer them, so they could never hurt me – or my grades –
again.*

Sixth grade is a little clearer for me. It was the
first year I remember my class being divided into two
math groups – one moving more quickly through
material, and the other moving somewhat slower. I also
remember being divided into three reading groups –
and relishing with pride my place in the top tier, the
honor of being taught by a seventh grade teacher, not
just a sixth grade one.

But when Mrs. Saltzbart, that seventh-grade
teacher, gave me a C+, I was devastated, embarrassed.
By sixth grade, a large portion of my sense of self
had been tied up with my grades. School comprised
the majority of my day: at eight hours a day, it was, in
essence, my full-time job. I wanted to be good at it, to
be recognized and praised just as anyone else wants in
their place of employment. The grades I earned were
my salary, doled out to me by teachers who seemed to
possess an infinite number of red letters to place atop
my tests, papers, and report cards. Though I wish I
could say that I enjoyed the mere act of learning, the
feeling of encountering something new and unusual
in this world, the real truth is that I was driven by the
competition for grades. My efforts were focused on
procuring them from teachers – and they were jealous
guardians. I learned to say the right words, organize my

essays, and show my work. I learned in middle school that I had to follow the rules the teachers set, do what they expected of me – or else I "failed" as a student, and to my mind, as a person.

If I didn't prove myself to be better than my classmates, then I didn't know who I was. I defined myself in relation to my friends' grades. I placed a lot of (too much) pressure on myself; my adolescence was marred by constant stress and struggle. All this competition came to a head in high school:

There I stood, a small slender figure at the front of a cavernous church. Mid-morning sunlight streamed through the stained glass windows in the full spectrum of color; under it, my audience turned green and blue, purple and gold. Their hands moved together in a disjointed wave of motion, giving ritual praise to the anthem just sung by the choir.

An imperceptible nod from my History teacher, and then with breath drawn like one about sing an operatic aria, I spoke. I was delivering my Valedictory address at the commencement of fours years spent (though I believed wasted) at St. Peter the Apostle High School. It was a moment when ordinary human beings would've felt proud – I was not. I felt steeped in, choked by mediocrity. There I was: delivering a mediocre speech, as the mediocre valedictorian of a mediocre class graduating from a mediocre high school.

The last words left my lips – it was a fine performance, if nothing else. Polite applause rang out; the sound was magnified by the echoing acoustics of the old (and might I add, also mediocre) church. For a moment, I felt almost hollow. Was this it? Was this all that I gained, after four years of working, worrying, stressing, struggling to be at the top of the class?

Then I realized the hollow feeling wasn't a lack of feeling anything, a negative state of emotion, but the lack of a single one. It was an emotion whose burden I'd carried

*for so long that I'd forgotten what it was like to be free of
it: resentment. I had won; I was no longer fighting to make
something of myself in an unimaginative and restrictive
educational environment. I was liberated – ready for college.
I longed for challenges, for intellectual rigor, for something
more than the sheer mediocrity that my life suffered from.*

*One day, I told myself, I'd write something worthy of
applause.*

In high school, I had believed that by proving
myself to be the best in my class, I could overcome
all the inadequacies I felt next to my friends: the
Valedictorianship was, for me, a way to finally be the
best, to be sure of who I was. Yet (not surprisingly),
I was still discontent. When the world is a race,
sometimes even winning it isn't enough – not if you are
only running against yourself.

What stands out to me in that passage, now, is
the bitterness of tone, the resentment I felt towards
all things academic. As I wrote this memoir a year
and a half ago, I was realizing just how futile the race
for grades was – I had been thrust from small, two-
hundred-large grammar and high schools into the
much larger Loyola, and I could no longer keep tabs
on everybody else's progress, rank, and grades. The
people at Loyola were far more diverse in interests,
the curriculum of the majors far too different, and the
possibilities for leadership so many, that I had to start
viewing my efforts in school in a different way. Instead
of regurgitating information, I was asked to start
thinking independently. Multiple choice and fill-in-the-
blank tests virtually disappeared; instead I was thinking
critically in essays and discussions.

My college-level writing classes were the best
example of this: no longer was I writing a paper
in one sitting and immediately turning it in for the

grade. I was forced to draft, workshop, and draft again. And then, I was asked to reflect on those drafts and workshops. Essentially, I had to shift my focus from the end product, to the *process* of writing – I did the same for my education. I had to stop memorizing, and begin internalizing a message that had to do with something other than competition.

This adjustment came slowly for me; I will confess that I do still hold something of an unhealthy preoccupation with whether I'm receiving a B+ or an A-. Yet, and I believe this is something more than coincidence, it was also in sophomore year that I was introduced to a world of literacy and education that was vastly different from my own, and in those differences, I saw all that I took for granted in my own education, most especially in the way competition shaped it.

My Writing Center class was the first in which I heard words like pedagogy and discourse; it was also that class that gave me statistics on literacy and illiteracy in Baltimore. I wish I could say that I was surprised when I heard that only about thirty-five percent of students in Baltimore graduated high school.[3] If I had been surprised, at least that would have shown naïveté or blissful ignorance on my part. But I wasn't. I honestly hadn't expected much more of Baltimore. Though I had only just started living in the city, the dismal state of the public school system was, and is, nothing short of notorious. I was cynical and conservative; I figured conditions like that were inevitable, so what could possibly be done to change them?

Yet I *was* surprised when it was suggested that the problem in those statistics wasn't from a lack of funding, or bad teachers, or even a poor work ethic on behalf of the students, but rather in a flaw in the process of education itself – the *pedagogy*, the

philosophy of the education. Here the concept of
discourse came alive for me, a word without a single
definition, but a dynamic one reflecting its need.
Discourse was, in one definition, the rules for writing in
a particular genre – history versus science, for instance.
Or, as it was more commonly used in class, discourse
implied all those hidden rules we have learned to think
and write in[4] – though the rules for writing may be
somewhat more overt, having been discussed time
and again in English classes throughout primary and
secondary education. I began to think of all the verbal,
written, and ideological structures I must have learned
in my own discourses, from the vocabulary I used with
connotations outside of the dictionary, to the ideals I
had adopted from the environment I grew up in.

Let me give a personal example: both of my parents
are college graduates. The upper-middle class nature
of my grammar school meant that most of my friends
were from similar backgrounds, with their parents
also being college graduates. When I left St. Matthias
School, I entered high school under the assumption
that I was always working towards an end goal of
attending college – a four-year college, specifically. I
thought all students in my high school were working
towards that same destination; yet, many of them opted
out of four-year colleges, and either sought immediate
employment, or attended two-year, local community
colleges. Furthermore, in the first few months of
freshman year, I began to hear numerous stories about
my old classmates dropping out of their schools and
pursuing alternate paths. At the time, I was frustrated
by this, not understanding why my peers didn't want
to pursue their education to the fullest extent. I was,
in many ways, a snob about my supposedly "superior"
college, placing formal, academic discourse and a

bachelor's degree in a more privileged position than that of pursuing an associate's degree, or entering the workforce.

Through the authors I was reading for the Writing Center class, I was beginning to see that such views were shaped by the privileges I had enjoyed previously – a strong grammar school education, and (despite my frustrations) a fair amount of success in the competitive environment that education created. With these musings in mind, I read an essay by Paulo Freire, *The Importance of the Act of Reading*, where he states: "Part of the context of my immediate world was the language universe of my elders, expressing their beliefs...and values which linked my world to a wider one whose existence I could not even suspect." Freire was writing about the effect of our discursive environment – and the way we view that environment – can have on us growing up. Students with a different educational history from my own, a different discourse regarding education, would be less inclined to pursue it longer than necessary.

Later in the essay, Freire also comments on effects of discourse in the student-teacher relationship: "Words should be laden with the meaning of the people's existential experience, and not of the teacher's experience." The implication, here, was that all too often we are taught, and teach, with bias. It's almost unavoidable; the discourses we belong to shape our very worldview. In and of itself, this bias is normal, but in a classroom, it can create conflicts. This is especially true, as Mary Soliday writes, with teachers and students from differing socioeconomic classes, and when the teachers assume that assimilation into academic discourse is the preferred option. Privileging academic discourse to the extent of overpowering another can hurt an individual's identity, and can negate a truly enlightening diversity in the classroom. This privileging can also extend beyond the classroom to culture; as we know it frequently happens that a minority culture, in all of its uniqueness, can be lost when the dominant culture either actively suppresses, or subversively assimilates the minorities into its own worldview.

As I went to compose the literacy memoir, I took these reflections, and transformed them into a history of competition; competition which I resented because of the futility I began to see in it. Yet, I also had to question my own personal success in school: did I perform so well because I possessed a similar background to my teachers?

As a result of the class, my interest in literacy as a social issue, and truly a social *justice* issue, expanded. In the spring semester of my sophomore year I applied for, and was accepted into, the SumServe program offered through Loyola's Center For Community Service and Justice (then known as the Center for Values and Service). SumServe would place me in a full-time position at a non-profit agency for the summer, along with weekly seminars on issues of inequality and justice.

The position I applied for was at The Learning Bank of C.O.I.L., Inc.: a center offering classes to adults (defined as learners aged sixteen and over) seeking a GED. Looking back on the process of applying, I can remember a great deal of nervousness; I wanted to be a part of the program, very badly. I had no concept of the challenge which lay ahead of me: my acceptance to The Learning Bank placement would become one of most educational – in a sense beyond mere schooling – experiences of my life.

There was a real dichotomy present in my experience at The Learning Bank. I knew I was exactly where I needed to be; from the moment I walked into

the three-story, open and spacious building, I knew
I wanted to work there. At the same time, I felt the
discomfort of an outsider – and I most certainly was.
The Learning Bank sat three blocks up from Martin
Luther King, Jr. Boulevard, on West Baltimore Street
– a neighborhood which has been documented in books
such as *The Corner* by Ed Burns and David Simon as a
hotbed of drug and gang-related activity.

Physically, the spot is an area of transition;
Baltimore Street is the traditional border between white
and black neighborhoods in Baltimore, a transition I
could clearly see as I made my left onto MLK every
afternoon going home. In front of me, I could see high-
rise office buildings leading into downtown Baltimore,
and the high-tech buildings of the University of
Maryland's medical school; in my rear view mirror,
there was naught but low-sitting row homes, and
boarded up shops, dotted with a few stores like A-1
Fried Chicken and the Dollar Beauty Supply. Yet, the
area around The Learning Bank was undergoing a
physical change: tall parking garages were in the middle
of their construction, and the light poles displayed
signs advertising the soon-to-come BioPark for UMD,
a bid by Baltimore to court the biomedical industry, to
boost its economy and create jobs. The only problem
was that few of the new jobs would be open to those
without a high school degree.

So there was The Learning Bank. Yes, its physical
location marks transition in Baltimore on a number of
levels, but inside its walls are dozens of learners who
are going through personal changes of their own. Some
are successful; in my first week, during that summer
of 2006, I witnessed a "graduation" ceremony for a
dozen learners who had just received their GEDs.
Some are not successful: when I returned this summer,
I recognized only a handful of faces from the group of

students I met last year, and the teachers told me such a turnover was not entirely due to successful graduation.

These were hard truths which I learned in pieces over that summer. There was no denying how different I was from the learners. Superficially, there was skin color; I can count on one hand the number of learners who weren't members of minority races. I was also younger than almost all of the learners, even if only by a few years. Under the surface, I had experienced a great deal of privilege in my education, having attended only private schools. I was somewhat embarrassed when I realized I was currently attending a college which probably cost more to attend per year than they were earning in wages.

Yet, I had to be careful in my assumptions; as the summer progressed, I learned more of the learner's stories, and found that each was unique. There was one man, tall and muscular, with a bright smile who introduced himself to me on my first day in an A-level classroom (which meant a first-to-third-grade reading level). He started a conversation with me, and I noticed how much thought he put into each sentence, as though he was searching an internal dictionary for the perfect word in each slot. He asked about Loyola; then, he told me that he had gone to college. He had attended a small, private university in Massachusetts on a basketball scholarship (in fact, he believed he had played against our team), and after playing for four years he graduated with a Bachelor of Arts degree – the same degree I was currently studying for. So why, I asked, was he at The Learning Bank? Then he told me, in his slow and deliberate way, about a severe car accident which damaged his brain. He was taking classes again to "brush-up" on his reading and arithmetic, in the hopes of going to college, again.

That was the first of many stories which broke down my presumptions. As the summer continued on, I became more and more emotionally involved with the learners, and in many ways began to forget our differences. The students, however, did not. I recall guiding a discussion about Jim Crow laws, one which was (to my great excitement) becoming fairly heated. In my eagerness to encourage the class to speak up, I mistakenly said "us" when talking about way the laws impacted Black Americans. I was not a part of that "us," as the awkward silence prevailing after my comment duly reminded me.

I always wanted to do more to help at The Learning Bank, and so Yvonne Butler, the Evening Coordinator and, at the time, C-level (sixth to eighth grade) teacher during the day, said I could assist in her first-period literature class. Since there were days when she had administrative duties to take care of, she figured it would be good for me to be there instead of her, and lead the class. Her classroom would be the site of some of my greatest mistakes, and subsequent lessons.

Of course, my intentions whenever I stepped to the front of a classroom were nothing but good. Yet, my idea of "good" was, as Freire had warned, biased by my own experience. In Freire's *Pedagogy of the Oppressed*, he writes that "many political and educational plans have failed because their authors designed them according to their own personal views of reality, never once taking into account... [those] to whom their origin was ostensibly directed." I would become a textbook example.

It began by grading a series of writing assignments from the men and women in Ms. Butler's class. I can only liken the experience to Mina Shaughnessy's first experience with a similar group of writers in the SEEK program at the City College of New York, detailed in her book *Errors and Expectations*:

"My students had just written their first essays, and...I now began to read them, hoping to be able to assess quickly the sort of task that lay ahead of us that semester. But the writing was so stunningly unskilled that I could not begin to define the task nor even sort out the difficulties. I could only sit there, reading and re-reading the alien papers, wondering what had gone wrong and trying to understand what I at this eleventh hour of my students' academic lives could do about it."

I use Shaughnessy's words, because I found them similar to my own, as written in my journal at the time:

"There are certain grammatical mistakes you expect to see, things like the misuse of commas, or mixing up your/you're, and its/it's; but there were mistakes in these essays (mere paragraphs, really) which I had never seen before. There were places where the learners wrote 'on' instead of 'and' – 'on' and 'in' I could see, but 'on' and 'and?' It's completely alien to me, and I don't even know where to begin in fixing it. Red marks on a page aren't going to instill these basic lessons, the knowledge of how to use quotes, and capitalize, and even just punctuate a sentence properly. I'm so used to these rules, it's as if I always knew them (and perhaps, because of how much I read, I did), teaching these learners feels akin to trying to teach someone who is tone-deaf how to sing."

There is a level of arrogance in my words that I cringe at, now. Teaching the "tone-deaf how to sing?" I assumed a hierarchy here, of my language over theirs. And I took a radical step to try and imbed my culture in theirs.

One afternoon, as I was discussing my findings in the learner's essays, Ms. Butler turned to me and said, quite casually: "You should take over class tomorrow.

Teach them something about grammar, so they can learn how to write, okay?" What to Ms. Butler sounded like an easy solution to my complaints, threw me into a panic. I was unprepared to become The Learning Bank's unofficial grammarian. So I turned to the only method I knew for teaching and learning grammar: the prescriptive, formal, repetitive method I knew of from grammar school. Perhaps, I thought, there was something to the use of the same word, grammar, for both. If I was working with learners on a seventh-grade reading level, then why shouldn't I use seventh-grade techniques? Concurrently with this conclusion, I also decided that the best way to learn was to show the learners their own mistakes. Reviewing their essays, I began to pick out the most common mistakes, such as double negatives, verb conjugations, etc. Using sentences taken, anonymously, from the learners' essays, I created a worksheet, and soon found myself presenting it in front of a classroom of men and woman whose very posture and expressions dared me to take authority.

As I wrote the first sentence on the blackboard, I was aware of a gentle moaning and groaning going through the class, as each learner found one of his or her own sentences on the worksheet. Now, I had left the authors of the sentences anonymous, assuming that would be enough to keep the learners from being embarrassed. I was wrong. The woman who wrote the sentence I was currently putting up on the board laughed nervously, betraying her authorship.

These signs alone should have warned me. Still, I continued on, convinced that in the end, they'd thank me for a thorough lesson in grammar. That first sentence I used in class appeared (to me) to be easy enough. "My man and me gone out after dinner." First, there was the use of an object pronoun in the sentence;

I figured, since that was a matter of substitution, it would be easier to start by discussing the difference between subject and object pronouns. I began to write the different subject-object pronouns on the board: *I* and *me*, *they* and *them*, etc. Then, the questions began – questions about subjects, objects, and pronouns. None of these terms were familiar to the men and women in the class. I tried to take each question individually, but I realized that I had assumed that the learners were working from the same base of knowledge I had possessed in seventh grade. It was the first time I realized my own bias, but not the last.

Flustered as I was, it wasn't the inquiries on the basic mechanics of grammar which really upset me. It was a single word, posed by the author of the offending sentence: "Why?"

I think it is important to note that she wasn't upset, she merely wanted to understand why using "I" was considered more correct than "me." She was a bright student, hardworking and very eager to learn. She never once questioned that she was wrong – I had said she was, and who was she to question as much?

I was caught off guard. Ms. Butler, in the back of the classroom, volunteered and answered while I stammered, unsure what to say.

"When you interview for a job," Ms. Butler spoke with authority, "they will expect you to sound a certain way - to write a certain way." For the learners, this explanation was enough. Most of them were seeking a GED to get better jobs, and they were willing to sacrifice their colloquialisms for that.

Still, *why* echoed in my brain, empty of reason or explanation. Questions began to roll through my mind: *Why does it matter? Why do we need an object and subject pronoun? Is the difference that essential to understanding the sentence? It gets the idea across, doesn't it?* Why couldn't they maintain their own, unique, and extraordinary local dialect? The "certain way" Ms. Butler spoke of was my upper-middle-class English, but it suddenly felt unfair to assume it was superior to the learner's. Weren't we just asking these learners to sacrifice their own unique discourse and take up another, to lose a unique part of their identity? Suddenly the thought occurred to me that I wasn't empowering my students; I was re-oppressing them.

Of course, English as a language is governed by rules, and these rules are what make it possible to communicate with one another. Play with language too much, and the common ground it creates is lost. If I say *up*, but mean *down*, how can I give directions with anyone else who thinks up is *up* and down is *down*?

In the English language, for example, it's known that the subject of an action comes before a verb, and the object after that – the subject-verb-object format is what Freire plays on when he writes about humanity's ontological vocation to be a subject. But language is also flexible, and one as widely spoken as English is constantly changing. Linguists are even starting to recognize this, studying African American Vernacular English (AAVE) as a language in its own right. English was once considered an "inferior" language, and, more importantly, the people who spoke it, the "lower class" were also inferior. Essentially, the battle of languages is a battle of classes: and I wondered if English-speakers were repeating the old class war between the French-speaking nobility and English-speaking serfs of the Middle Ages, with AAVE looked down upon as English once was? Is it *ever* fair to judge an individual based on the language he or she speaks?

After my disastrous grammar lesson ended, I felt permanently unsettled. So I began to sit back and listen. I let the conversation of the learners wash over me, and let them become the teachers.

The realizations and insights were small; at first, I noticed the way the Baltimore accent influenced their speech — or *Ballimer*, as they pronounced it. And then, I noticed why their "ands" and "ons" were being switched: the confusion wasn't about mistaking a preposition for a conjunction, but about simply being an inexperienced speller. Phonetically, the Baltimorean "and" was like "on," and the learners I taught were simply spelling by sounding it out – as we've all been told in elementary school.

Then, there were the broader topics. Discussions about W.E.B. DuBois and Booker T. Washington, and their competing views on education revealed just how real slavery and segregation still were to the learners. The debate between Washington's Tuskegee Institute and its vocational philosophy of education, and DuBois's more all-around, liberal arts approach to education highlighted the struggle within the discourse of Black Americans today. Do they pursue economic success within the structure of society today, or do they fight against that structure and seek economic success through the change? I saw the imprint of slavery even today, a century and a half later, in the struggle of these individuals to overcome the lack of opportunities and privileges that I had received so freely, and had looked upon with such distaste.

When I taught again, I could understand the learner's frustration. I could understand when a frustrated woman asked me, "When did you learn about this infinitives stuff?" I also understood when my response of middle school earned a disgruntled comment about that not being covered in *her* middle school. I could see the differences in our discourses, between St. Matthias and a public school in Baltimore. And I no longer assumed that I knew what was best for the learners. My lesson plans responded to what they wanted to learn, and their questions.

Again, I began to re-evaluate my educational memories, and all the credit I had given myself for earning strong grades. What if I had to baby-sit younger siblings every afternoon while my mother worked (as one learner told me often happened to her)? Would I have completed my homework so thoroughly, so completely then? What if my parents hadn't given me the chance to be involved with so many extracurricular activities – where would I have turned to for entertainment? I was suddenly aware of my privilege in a very keen way, suffering from what I would hear described as "white guilt."

Always needing to be active, I couldn't suffer with this guilt for long before I was seeking ways to turn it into something with purpose. Freire, observing a similar phenomenon, writes that:

"Discovering himself to be an oppressor may cause considerable anguish [to an individual], but it does not necessarily lead to solidarity with the oppressed.... Solidarity requires that one enter into the situation of those with whom one is solidary...[and] true solidarity means fighting at their side to transform the objective reality which has made them [the oppressed] 'beings for another.'"

In short, I needed to face the privilege I had been given, and somehow sacrifice it. Only in seeing myself as a part of the learners, and taking part in what Freire calls a "dialog of equals" with them, could I work to end the oppression.

This discourse-crossing dialog is the most critical aspect to Freire's concept of enacting revolution. While I cannot forget all that I have learned throughout my education, I can forget the notion that my education is supposed to be "superior." I can come

face to face with a learner, and listen without judging.
What I cannot believe is that I possess the "solution" all
on my own; I must realize that I am only a single part
of a solution which must ultimately originate within the
oppressed. Otherwise, my "solution" is just a continued
form of charity - not *caritas*.

It is not easy for me (and I suspect many others)
to remain aware of a lack of control in these
circumstances. One wants to believe that he or she can
change the world, that he or she can single-handedly
stop injustice, a superman or -woman delivering
salvation to the oppressed. Yet, the whole point of
Freire's subjectivity is to be a person creating his or
her own action. If I try to rescue the world, I reduce
everyone else in it to objects. So it cannot be from
me that the learners find their voice to cry out for
revolution.

Now, I am only twenty-one years old, and I do not
pretend to know all there is to know about injustice,
and fighting it. But my hope is for this book, for these
stories which I present to you as a sort of dialog, is
simple: that you, too, can learn to cast aside your pride,
your assumptions, and your past, and come to view
these narratives as those of equals – for we are all
equal in our humanity. We all once crowded around that
single torch which Prometheus gave to us, and saw in it
a future bright and burning.

Perhaps, we can emulate Prometheus's example,
still. When he brought fire to humankind, he was
giving a tool, leveling the ground, so-to-speak, between
Mount Olympus and humanity's humble beginnings.
We are the ones who seized upon fire, and caused a
revolution. The learners here are only just beginning to
light their torches, and their fires can only grow.

&Endnotes

1. Qtd in Stephen Harold Riggins, "The Rhetoric of Othering," The Language and Politics of Exclusion: Others in Discourse (California: SAGE Publications, 1997), 5.

2. There is something interesting to be said for the fact that these revolutions all happened to cultures which were once the oppressed, but later gained power and misused it. For an interesting commentary on cultural assimilation, see Freire, Pedagogy, 150-166.

3. "Graduation Profiles" Education Week 26, no. 40 (2007): par 8, http://www.edweek.org/ew/article s/2007/06/12/40gradprofiles.h26.html

4. Sarah Mills, Discourse (New York: Routledge, 1997), 5.

&Bibliography

Burns, Edward, and David Simon. *The Corner: A Year in the Life of an Inner City Neighborhood*. New York: Broadway Books, 1998.

Freire, Paulo. *Pedagogy of the Oppressed*. Translated by Myra Bergman Ramos. New York: Continuum, 1982.

Freire, Paulo. "The Importance of the Act of Reading." *The Journal of Education* 165, no. 1 (1983): 7-12.

"Graduation Profiles" *Education Week* 26, no. 40 (2007). http://www.edweek.org/ew/articles/200 7/06/12/40gradprofiles.h26.html.

Hourigan, Maureen M. *Literacy as Social Exchange*. New York: State University of New York Press, 1994.

Mills, Sarah. *Discourse*. New York: Routledge, 1997.

Riggins, Stephen Harold. *The Language and Politics of Exclusion: Others in Discourse*. California: SAGE Publications, 1997.

Soliday, Mary. "The Politics of Difference: Towards a Pedagogy of Reciprocity." In *Writing in Multicultural Settings*, edited by Johnella E. Butler, Juan C. Guerra, and Carol Severino. 261-286. New York: Modern Language Association, 1997.

Zerubavel, Eviatar. "Islands of Meaning." *Inside Social Life: Readings in Sociological Psychology and Microsociolog*, edited by Spencer E. Cahill. 16-23. Los Angeles:Roxbury Publishing Company, 2004.

The following is a couple of books which allow further exploration into literacy and education, including some works listed cited above. For those interested in education and politics, I wholeheartedly recommend:

Freire, Paulo. *The Politics of Education: Culture, Power, and Liberation.* Translated by Donald Macedo. New York: Bergin & Garvey, 1985.

For literacy, writing and its impact on culture, and cultural exchange, I recommend:

Yagelski, Robert P. *Literacy Matters: Writing and Reading and the Social Self.* New York: Teacher's College Press, 2000.

The future of publishing...today!

Apprentice House is the country's only campus-based, student-staffed book publishing company. Directed by professors and industry professionals, it is a nonprofit activity of the Communication Department at Loyola College in Maryland.

Using state-of-the-art technology and an experiential learning model of education, Apprentice House publishes books in untraditional ways. This dual responsibility as publishers and educators creates an unprecedented collaborative environment among faculty and students, while teaching tomorrow's editors, designers, and marketers.

Outside of class, progress on book projects is carried forth by the AH Book Publishing Club, a co-curricular campus organization supported by Loyola College's Office of Student Activities.

Student Project Team for *Prometheus's Torch*
    Elizabeth Watson '08
    Brielle Fiorillo '08

Eclectic and provocative, Apprentice House titles intend to entertain as well as spark dialogue on a variety of topics.

Financial contributions to sustain the press's work are welcomed. Contributions are tax deductible to the fullest extent allowed by the IRS.

To learn more about Apprentice House books or to obtain submission guidelines, please visit www.ApprenticeHouse.com

Apprentice House
Communication Department
Loyola College in Maryland
4501 N. Charles Street
Baltimore, MD 21210
Ph: 410-617-5265 • Fax: 410-617-5040
info@apprenticehouse.com